D1552726

Pittsburgh Series in Bibliography

DASHIELL HAMMETT

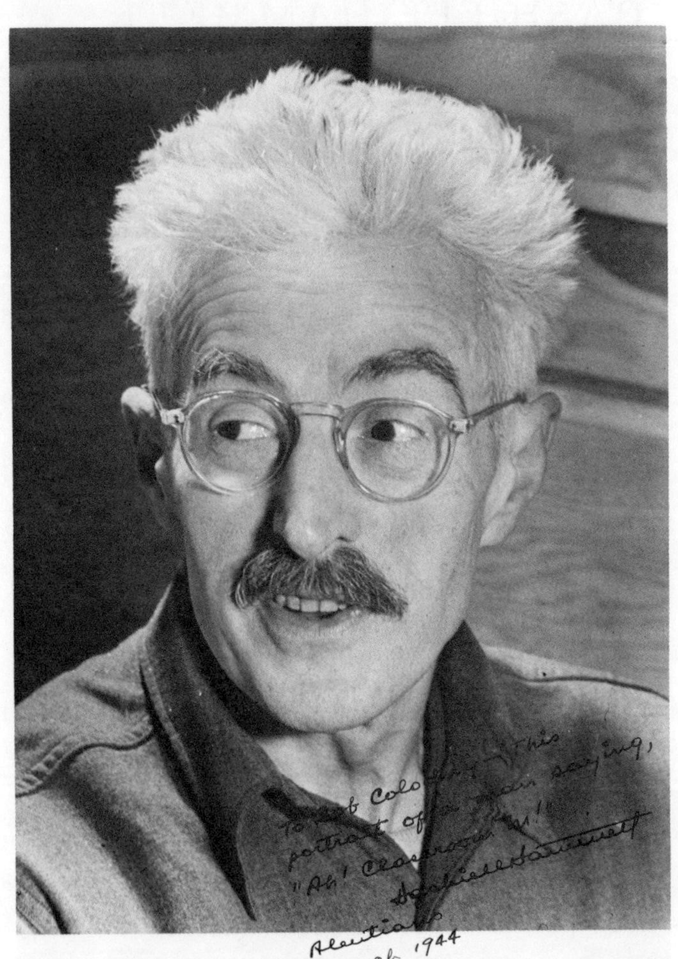
Aleutians
March 1944

Dashiell Hammett

A DESCRIPTIVE BIBLIOGRAPHY

Richard Layman

UNIVERSITY OF
PITTSBURGH PRESS
1979

For Nancy S. Layman

Published by the University of Pittsburgh Press, Pittsburgh, Pa. 15260

Feffer and Simons, Inc., London
Manufactured in the United States of America

Library of Congress Cataloging in Publication Data

Layman, Richard, 1947–
Dashiell Hammett: a descriptive bibliography.

(Pittsburgh series in bibliography)
Includes index.
1. Hammett, Dashiell, 1894–1961—Bibliography.
I. Title. II. Series.
Z8385.L39 [PS3515.A4347] 016.813'5'2 78-53600
ISBN 0-8229-3394-2

The photograph of the dust jacket for A2.1.a was furnished through the courtesy of the Humanities Research Center Library, The University of Texas at Austin, Austin, Texas.

Contents

Acknowledgments

HAMMETT bibliography started with William F. Nolan. His *Dashiell Hammett: A Casebook* (Santa Barbara: McNally & Loftin, 1969) has been the sole book-length study of Hammett, and his scholarship has laid a solid foundation for my work. Mr. Nolan has been most generous with assistance on this project and has provided valuable counsel.

Special thanks are due the following who were uncommonly helpful: Muriel Alexander, William Blackbeard, Robert Colodny, David Fechheimer, Glenda G. Fedricci, William Glackin, William Godshalk, Adrian Goldstone, Anita Luccioni, William H. Lyles, Susan Manakul, Otto Penzler, Rhonda W. Rabon, Robert L. Samsell, E. E. Spitzer, Michael Sutherland, and Cara L. White. I wish to express my gratitude to the members of the Editorial Board of the Pittsburgh Series in Bibliography: Matthew J. Bruccoli, General Editor; William R. Cagle; Charles W. Mann; and Joel Myerson.

Institutional libraries and their staffs have made my work possible. Chief among them are the University of California at Los Angeles Library, Duke University Library, The Lilly Library at Indiana University, the Library of Congress, the Berg Collection and the general library at the New York Public Library, the University of North Carolina Library at Chapel Hill, Occidental College Library, the San Francisco Academy of Comic Art, the San Francisco Public Library, and the Thomas Cooper Library at the University of South Carolina.

Finally, thanks are due the bookdealers, too numerous to mention, who are the real bibliographical detectives.

Introduction

DASHIELL Hammett's active writing career lasted barely twelve years, from the beginning of 1922 to the end of 1933. In that time he revolutionized American detective fiction with his stories in pulp magazines and produced five novels that have been hailed as classics of the genre. He was hardworking and ambitious. In the twenties his stories were published at the rate of one every six weeks; when he turned to the novel, he wrote his first four books in less than four years. Then after publication of *The Thin Man* he quit. Twenty years later he explained: "I stopped writing because I found I was repeating myself. It is the beginning of the end when you discover you have style" (D 422).

This bibliography is intended as a record of how that style was developed in print and how it was utilized.

FORMAT

Section A lists chronologically all books wholly or substantially by Hammett, including all editions in English. At the end of this section there is an AA supplemental list of collections of Hammett's writing. The numbering system for Section A designates the edition and printing for each entry. Thus for *Red Harvest, A 1.2.b* indicates that the entry describes the first book by Hammett *(1)* in its second edition *(2),* second printing *(b).* In story collections first book appearances are marked with an asterisk.

Section B lists chronologically all titles not listed in Section A that contain material by Hammett published for the first time in a book. The first printings only of these items are described. Memoirs that quote, or seem to quote, Hammett in recollected anecdotes have been omitted, although Lillian Hellman's memoirs have been included because of their importance. Miss Hellman's plays that contain speeches or revisions by Hammett have been omitted (in *An Unfinished Woman,* for example, Miss Hellman recounts how a speech in *The Autumn Garden* was written by Hammett [p. 268]).

Section C lists chronologically all first appearances of Hammett's work in magazines. This section posed particular difficulties because of the nature of the magazines for which Hammett wrote. Pulp magazines have rarely been preserved in a systematic way, and it has been impossible to locate copies of some of Hammett's stories in their first magazine publication. Entries were verified against a card file Hammett kept of his published work for copyright renewal. Page numbers and volume numbers have been included in this section only when they could be verified. Anonymous book reviews in the *Saturday Review* have been attributed to Hammett on the basis of the magazine's inventory of books sent to reviewers. If Hammett was sent a book and an anonymous review of that book later appeared in *Saturday Review,* it has been assumed that Hammett wrote the review.

Section D lists all first newspaper appearances of Hammett's work as well as interviews and public statements. Items are presented chronologically except that his book-review column, comic strip, and his *Adakian* articles are each grouped together. It is virtually certain that a number of interviews have not yet been located. A supplementary section DD lists public letters or petitions signed by Hammett.

Section E lists movies for which Hammett provided the original story or script material.

Section F lists miscellaneous material—dust jacket blurbs by Hammett and a form letter circulated under his name.

From no earlier than 1922 until May 1926, Hammett was advertising manager for Albert S. Samuels Jewelry Company. The Samuels ads that appeared in the *San Francisco Examiner* during that time are listed in *Appendix 1.* Samuels did not advertise exclusively in the *Examiner,* nor did Hammett write all of the ads. But Hammett did write some of them and participated in conferences at which ad material was discussed and approved.

Appendix 2 lists radio plays based on Hammett's work. His contract with MGM did not allow him to sell the right to adapt his characters or his work to other media unless he himself wrote the adaptation. So Hammett was credited with writing radio plays he never saw but did profit from. It cannot be proved that Hammett ever wrote a radio play.

Appendix 3 lists movies, television programs, and stage plays based on Hammett's work, but in which he had no hand.

Appendix 4 lists newspaper syndication of previously published works by Hammett.

Appendix 5 lists the compiler's notes on unlocated material.

Appendix 6 lists selected references, primarily bibliographical.

TERMS AND METHODS

Edition. All the copies of a book printed from a single setting of type—including all reprintings from standing type, from plates, or by photo-offset processes.

Printing. All the copies of a book printed at one time (without removing the type or plates from the press). Printings exist within editions.[1]

The form of entry for first English editions or printings is somewhat condensed from the full form provided for American editions.

Dust jackets for Section A entries have been described in detail because they are part of the original publication effort and sometimes provide information about how the book was marketed. There is, of course, no certainty that a jacket now on a copy of a book was always on it.

1. No states or issues have been noted in Hammett's books.

For binding-cloth designations I have used the method proposed by Tanselle.[2] Most of these cloth grains are illustrated in Jacob Blanck, ed., *Bibliography of American Literature* (New Haven: Yale University Press, 1955–).

Colors for binding and dust jackets are designated as simply as possible. National Bureau of Standards Centroid color names and numbers have not been used. It is rarely—if ever—possible to designate exactly the color for the binding cloth of a fifty-year-old book or its dust jacket. Oxidation and fading change colors, and it is the compiler's feeling that use of Centroid color designations under such circumstances gives a false sense of precision.

The spines of bindings and dust jackets are printed horizontally unless otherwise stipulated.

In the descriptions of title pages, bindings, and dust jackets, the color of the lettering is always black, unless otherwise stipulated. The style of type is roman, unless otherwise stipulated.

The term *perfect binding* refers to books in which the pages are held together with adhesive along the back edge after the folds have been trimmed off, as with most paperbacks.

Book descriptions do not include leaf thickness or sheet bulk because there is no case for Hammett in which these measurements are required to differentiate printings.

Locations are given in the National Union Catalog symbols—with these exceptions:

BL: British Library
Bod: Bodleian Library
OP: Collection of Otto Penzler
RL: Collection of Richard Layman
SFACA: San Francisco Academy of Comic Art

For paperbacks the serial number provided is that of the first printing. Paperback publishers often change the serial number in later printings; this information has been noted in this bibliography.

It is desirable in bibliographical description to avoid end-of-line hyphens in transcriptions. Because of word lengths and a measured line, however, it is impossible to satisfy this requirement. End-of-line hyphens have been avoided wherever possible, and always where a hyphen would create ambiguity.

A bibliography is outdated the day it goes to the printer. Addenda and corrigenda are earnestly solicited.

Columbia, South Carolina
10 October 1978

2. G. Thomas Tanselle, "The Specifications of Binding Cloth," *The Library*, 21 (September 1966), 246–247.

A. Separate Publications

A 1 RED HARVEST

A 1.1.a
First edition, first printing (1929)

DASHIELL HAMMETT

RED HARVEST

New York · ALFRED · A · KNOPF · *London*
19 29

A 1.1.a: 7 3/8" × 5 1/8"

COPYRIGHT 1927, 1929 BY ALFRED A. KNOPF, INC. *Manufactured in the United States of America*

[1–18]^{8}

[i–xii] [1–3] 4–13 [14] 15–25 [26] 27–37 [38] 39–49 [50] 51–60 [61] 62–70 [71] 72–81 [82] 83–87 [88] 89–99 [100] 101–107 [108] 109–117 [118] 119–128 [129] 130–137 [138] 139–146 [147] 148–157 [158] 159–164 [165] 166–177 [178] 179–183 [184] 185–191 [192] 193–202 [203] 204–211 [212] 213–225 [226] 227–235 [236] 237–244 [245] 246–250 [251] 252–259 [260] 261–270 [271–276]

Contents: pp. i–iv: blank; p. v.: half title; p. vi: card page; p. vii: title; p. viii: copyright; p. ix: dedication; p. x: blank; pp. xi–xii: contents; p. 1: half title; p. 2: blank; pp. 3–270: text, headed 'CHAPTER I | *A Woman in Green and a Man in Gray'*; p. 271: colophon; pp. 272–276: blank.

Typography and paper: 5⁷/₁₆″ (5⁵/₈″) × 3¹/₂″. 29 or 30 lines per page. Running heads: rectos, chapter titles; versos, 'RED HARVEST'. Wove paper.

Binding: Deep red V cloth (smooth). Front: stamped very yellow skull and crossbones within stamped black single-rule frame. Spine: 5 panels with stamped decorations in yellow and black against red background; '[in red against black panel] RED | HARVEST | DASHIELL | HAMMET | [in yellow against red panel] ALFRED • A • | KNOPF'. Back: stamped black rectangle outlining Borzoi seal in lower right-hand corner. White wove sized endpapers. Top and bottom edges trimmed. Top edge stained green.

Dust jacket: White paper printed predominately in black. Front: '[within white panel bordered by orange single-rule frame against black background with vertical orange and red devices on either side] RED | HAR- | VEST | A THRILLING | DETECTIVE | STORY | by | DASHIELL | HAMMETT'. Spine: '[against black background within orange single-rule frame on 3 sides, printed in white] RED | HARVEST | [device] | DASHIEL | HAMMETT | BORZOI | [Borzoi seal] | BOOKS | ALFRED•A | KNOPF'. Back: '[against white background within orange double-rules frame] RED | HARVEST | DASHIELL | HAMMETT | [17 lines of blurbs from *The Bookman, The Outlook,* and *The Chicago Post*] | ALFRED A. KNOPF | PUBLISHER, NEW YORK | [Borzoi seal]'. Front flap: list of Borzoi mysteries, beginning with Virgil Markham. Back flap: list from front flap continued, beginning with J. S. Fletcher, *The Middle Temple Murder.*

Publication: Unknown number of copies of the first printing. $2.50. Published 1 February 1929. Copyright 1 February 1929. Copyright #A7441.

Printing: Plates, printing, and binding by H. Wolff Estate.

Note: *Red Harvest* was first published in *Black Mask* in 4 parts; see C 77, C 80, C 83, and C 86.

Locations: BL ('26 JAN 1929'); Bod ('SEP 24 1929'); InU; RL.

A 1.1.b
Second printing: New York: Knopf, 1930.

Copyright page: *'Published February, 1929 | Second Printing March, 1930'.*

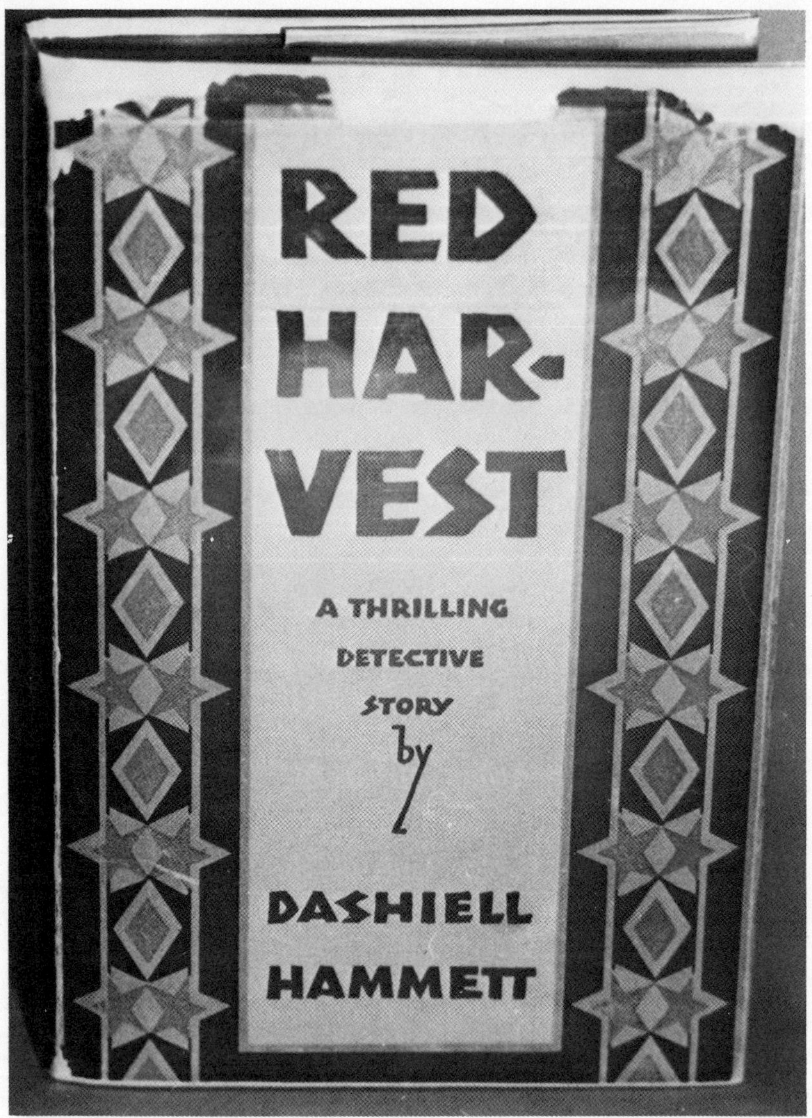

Dust jacket front for A 1.1.a

A 1.1.c
Third printing (1931)

[decorated rule] | RED HARVEST | BY | DASHIELL HAMMETT | *Author of* | THE DAIN CURSE | THE MALTESE FALCON | GROSSET & DUNLAP | PUBLISHERS NEW YORK | [decorated rule]

Copyright page: 'Published February, 1929 | Second Printing March, 1930 | Third Printing March, 1931'.

Note: Pocket Books edition (A 1.2.a) notes 3 printings by Grosset & Dunlap.

A 1.1.d
Fourth printing: Dashiell Hammett Omnibus. New York: Knopf, 1935.

See AA 1.

Note: Copyright page notes that *Red Harvest* has been *'Reprinted five times'*.

A 1.1.e
Fifth printing: The Complete Dashiell Hammett. New York: Knopf, 1942.

See AA 1.c.

Note: Pocket Books edition (A 1.2.a) notes 2 printings.

A 1.1.f
Sixth printing: (1943)

[decorated rule] | RED HARVEST | BY | DASHIELL HAMMETT | *Author of* THE DAIN CURSE | THE MALTESE FALCON | [6-line notice about wartime conservation of materials] | GROSSET & DUNLAP | PUBLISHERS NEW YORK | [decorated rule]

1943.

A 1.1.g
Seventh printing: New York: Knopf, 1947.

Black Widow Thriller. Not seen.

A 1.2.a
Second edition, first printing (1943)

[within shaded single-rule frame] RED | HARVEST | *by Dashiell Hammett* | THE BLAKISTON COMPANY, Philadelphia | *Distributed by* | POCKET ['BOOKS' in hollow letters] BOOKS INC. [kangaroo device] NEW YORK, 20, N.Y.

Copyright page: 'Pocket BOOKS *edition published December, 1943* | 1ST PRINTING [7 dots] OCTOBER, 1943'.

#241.

Note: Permabook edition (A 1.4.a) notes 5 printings by Pocket Books.

A 1.2.b
Second edition, second printing (1943?)

[within shaded single-rule frame] RED | HARVEST | *by Dashiell Hammett* | READER'S LEAGUE OF AMERICA

1943? New York.

A 1.3
Third edition: The Dashiell Hammett Omnibus. London, Toronto, Melbourne, Sydney, Wellington: Cassell, 1950.

See AA 3.

A 1.4.a
Fourth edition, first printing (1956)

RED HARVEST | [decorated rule] | by DASHIELL HAMMETT | [anchor device] | PERMABOOKS • NEW YORK

Copyright page: 'PERMABOOK edition published July, 1956 | 1st printing [27 dots] May, 1956'.

#M3043.

A 1.4.b
Fourth edition, second printing

Not seen.

A 1.4.c
Fourth edition, third printing (1961)

[within 3-sided single-rule frame] DASHIELL HAMMETT | [within another 3-sided single-rule frame] RED HARVEST | [within another 3-sided single-rule frame interrupted on top by anchor device] PERMABOOKS • NEW YORK

Copyright page: 'PERMABOOK edition published July, 1956 | 3rd printing [23 dots] January, 1961'.

#M4201.

A 1.5
Fifth edition? London: Hamilton (Stafford), 1958.

Not seen.

A 1.6.a
Sixth edition, first printing (1963)

DASHIELL HAMMETT | RED HARVEST | [tapered rule] | PENGUIN BOOKS

Copyright page: 'Published in Penguin Books 1963'.

Harmondsworth. #1888.

A 1.6.b
Sixth edition, second printing (1975)

Dashiell Hammett | RED HARVEST | Pan Books Ltd London and Sydney

Copyright page: 'This edition published 1975'.

A 1.7
Seventh edition: The Novels of Dashiell Hammett. New York: Knopf, 1965.

See AA 4.

A 1.8
Eighth edition (1968)

Red Harvest | [rule] | DASHIELL HAMMETT | A DELL BOOK

Copyright page: 'First Dell printing—June 1968'.

New York. #7291.

A 1.9
Ninth edition (1972)

Red Harvest | DASHIELL HAMMETT | [Vintage seal] | VINTAGE BOOKS | *A Division of Random House* | NEW YORK

Copyright page: 'First Vintage Books Edition, October 1972'.

#V-828.

A 1.10
Tenth edition (1974)

Dashiell Hammett | RED HARVEST | UNIFORM EDITION | [woman with bow] | CASSELL • LONDON

Copyright page: 'First published in this edition 1974'.

A 2 THE DAIN CURSE

A 2.1.a
First edition, first printing (1929)

DASHIELL HAMMETT

THE DAIN CURSE

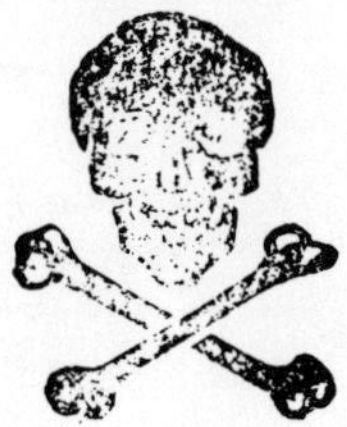

New York · ALFRED·A·KNOPF · *London*
1929

A 2.1.a: 7³/₈″ × 5¹/₈″

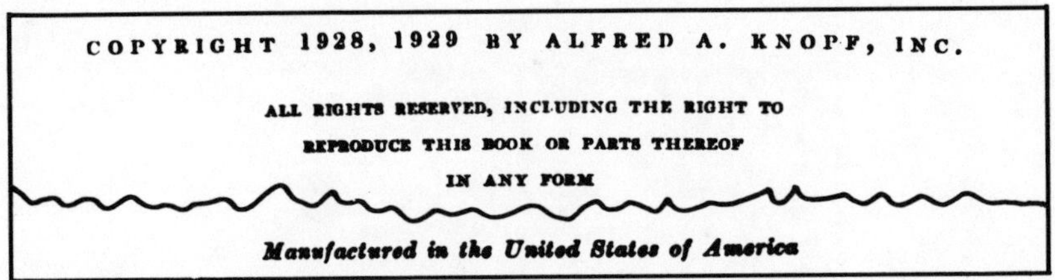
COPYRIGHT 1928, 1929 BY ALFRED A. KNOPF, INC.

ALL RIGHTS RESERVED, INCLUDING THE RIGHT TO
REPRODUCE THIS BOOK OR PARTS THEREOF
IN ANY FORM

Manufactured in the United States of America

[1–18]^{8}

[i–x] [1–3] 4–11 [12] 13–19 [20] 21–33 [34] 35–39 [40] 41–55 [56] 57–62 [63] 64–74 [75] 76–79 [80–83] 84–93 [94] 95–107 [108] 109–120 [121] 122–134 [135–137] 138–148 [149] 150–159 [160] 161–170 [171] 172–183 [184] 185–193 [194] 195–203 [204] 205–217 [218] 219–232 [233] 234–246 [247] 248–261 [262] 263–272 [273–278]

Contents: pp. i–ii: blank; p. iii: half title; p. iv: card page; p. v: title; p. vi: copyright; p. vii: dedication; p. viii: blank; pp. ix–x: contents; p. 1: part title, 'PART ONE: THE DAINS'; p. 2: blank; pp. 3–79: text, headed 'CHAPTER I | *Eight Diamonds';* p. 80: blank; p. 81: part title, 'PART TWO: THE TEMPLE'; p. 82: blank; pp. 83–134: text; p. 135: part title, 'PART THREE: QUESADA'; p. 136: blank, pp. 137–272: text; p. 273: colophon; pp. 274–278: blank.

Typography and paper: $5^{9}/_{16}''$ (6″) × $3^{5}/_{8}''$. 31 or 32 lines per page. Running heads: rectos, chapter titles; versos, 'THE DAIN CURSE'. Wove paper.

Binding: Medium yellow V cloth (smooth). Front: stamped dark reddish orange skull and crossbones within stamped dark reddish brown single-rule frame. Spine: 5 panels with stamped decorations in brown and red; '[in yellow against brown panel] THE DAIN | CURSE | DASHIELL | HAMMETT | [in red against yellow panel] ALFRED • A • | KNOPF'. Back: stamped brown rectangle outlining Borzoi seal in lower right-hand corner. White sized endpapers. Top and bottom edges trimmed. Top edge stained brown. Variant binding noted in brown cloth.

Dust jacket: Front: '[drawing of man and bird in yellow, white, and black against orange background] THE | DAIN | CURSE | [in green] A BORZOI MYSTERY STORY | BY | DASHIELL HAMMETT | AUTHOR OF | RED HARVEST | [Borzoi seal] | [drawing signed 'F.H. Horvath']'. Spine: '[against orange background] THE | DAIN | CURSE | BY | DASHIELL | HAMMETT | [continuation of drawing on front] | [in white] ALFRED A. | KNOPF'. Back: '[against white background within decorated orange frame] THE | DAIN CURSE | By | DASHIELL HAMMETT | [11-line plot outline] | Alfred A. Knopf [Borzoi seal] Publisher, N.Y.'. Front flap: 'By Dashiell Hammett | RED HARVEST | [20 lines of blurbs about *Red Harvest*] | [Borzoi seal]'. Back flap: '*The Detective Stories of* | J. S. Fletcher | [40-line list of titles with prices]'.

Publication: Unknown number of copies of the first printing. $2.00. Published 19 July 1929. Copyright 19 July 1929. Copyright #A11359.

Printing: Plates, printing, and binding by H. Wolff Estate.

Note 1: *The Dain Curse* was first published in *Black Mask* in 4 parts; see C 92, C 97, C 101, and C 103.

Note 2: 'dopped in' at 260.19 is often given as a first-printing point, but all copies of the first edition examined have the misprint.

Locations: RL; TxU (dj).

The Detective Stories of
J. S. FLETCHER
THE MIDDLE TEMPLE MURDER*
THE TALLEYRAND MAXIM
THE PARADISE MYSTERY*
DEAD MEN'S MONEY
THE CHESTERMARKE INSTINCT
THE ORANGE-YELLOW DIAMOND
THE BOROUGH TREASURER*
THE HERAPATH PROPERTY*
SCARHAVEN KEEP
THE RAYNER-SLADE AMALGAMATION
RAVENSDENE COURT
THE MIDDLE OF THINGS
THE LOST MR. LINTHWAITE*
EXTERIOR TO THE EVIDENCE
THE MARKENMORE MYSTERY*
THE KING VERSUS WARGRAVE
THE MAZAROFF MYSTERY
THE TIME-WORN TOWN
THE WOLVES AND THE LAMB
THE ANNEXATION SOCIETY
FALSE SCENT
THE AMARANTH CLUB
THE KANG-HE VASE
THE CARTWRIGHT GARDENS MURDER
THE GREAT BRIGHTON MYSTERY
SEA FOG
THE MISSING CHANCELLOR
THE MORTOVER GRANGE AFFAIR
THE GREEN ROPE
THE PASSENGER TO FOLKESTONE
THE STRANGE CASE OF MR. HENRY MARCHMONT
THE MURDER IN THE PALLANT
COBWEB CASTLE
THE WRISTMARK
THE HOUSE IN TUESDAY MARKET
THE MATHESON FORMULA
$2.00 EACH
*$1.00 IN THE BORZOI POCKET BOOKS
Other volumes in preparation
THE
DAIN CURSE
By
DASHIELL HAMMETT
A destructive fate pursues Gabrielle Leggett wherever she goes: it annihilates her home, penetrates into the new thought temple where she takes refuge, brings her wedding-trip to a tragic end and drives her to the verge of insanity. Following the girl's amazing career by devious and unprecedented ways of his own, Mr. Hammett's unequalled detective succeeds in vanquishing the curse that hangs over Gabrielle's head and corners what is perhaps one of the most remarkable criminals in fiction.
Alfred A. Knopf
BORZOI BOOKS
Publisher, N.Y.
THE DAIN CURSE
BY
DASHIELL HAMMETT
ALFRED A. KNOPF
THE
DAIN
CURSE
By Dashiell Hammett
RED HARVEST
"The liveliest detective story that has been published in a decade."—Herbert Asbury
"It is a fast-stepping melodramatic tale, told in choice underworld vernacular by the sleuth himself, a book which we recommend as fiction . . . of a genuinely fresh and entertaining quality."—The New York Sun
"Here is the best of a batch of current detective stories and mystery thrillers. It is the best because it is so startlingly original. There has never been a detective story like it."—The Cleveland Plain Dealer
"When it is written by a man who plainly knows his underworld and can make it come alive for his readers, when the action is exciting, and the conversation racy and amusing—well, you'll want to read it. . . We recommend this one without reservation. We gave it A plus before we'd finished the first chapter."—The Outlook
BORZOI BOOKS

Dust jacket for A 2.1.a

A2.1.b
Second printing

Not seen.

A2.1.c
Third printing: New York: Knopf, 1929.

Copyright page: 'Published July, 1929 | Second Printing August, 1929 | Third Printing August, 1929'.

A2.1.d
Fourth printing, first English publication (1930)

DASHIELL HAMMETT

THE DAIN CURSE

New York · ALFRED · A · KNOPF · *London*

19 30

A2.1.d: 7³/₈" × 5¹/₈"

Copyright page: 'FIRST PUBLISHED, 1930, BY ALFRED A. KNOPF, LTD. | *Printed in the United States of America*'.

$[1\text{–}17]^8\ [18]^6$

[i–x] [1–3] 4–11 [12] 13–19 [20] 21–33 [34] 35–39 [40] 41–55 [56] 57–62 [63] 64–74 [75] 76–79 [80–83] 84–93 [94] 95–107 [108] 109–120 [121] 122–134 [135–137] 138–148 [149] 150–159 [160] 161–170 [171] 172–183 [184] 185–193 [194] 195–203 [204] 205–217 [218] 219–232 [233] 234–246 [247] 248–261 [262] 263–272 [273–274]

Binding: Orange cloth. Front: black skull and crossbones in upper right-hand corner. Spine: '[thick rule] | [thin rule] | THE | DAIN | CURSE | DASHIELL | HAMMETT | KNOPF | [thin rule] | [thick rule]'. Back. Borzoi seal in reverse printing in lower right-hand corner.

Dust jacket: Not seen.

Publication: Published January 1930. 7s. 6d.

Note 1: Card page, [iv], lists date of *The Dain Curse* as 1930.

Note 2: Copyright page of 1945 Pocket Books edition (A 2.2.a) notes that this English publication was first printed in November 1929 and reprinted in January 1930.

Locations: BL ('8 JAN 30'); Bod ('FEB 18 1930').

A 2.1.e
Fifth printing (1930)

THE | DAIN CURSE | BY | DASHIELL HAMMETT | AUTHOR OF | RED HARVEST | [device] | GROSSET & DUNLAP | PUBLISHERS NEW YORK

Copyright page: 'Third Printing August, 1929'.

1930.

Note: Copyright page of 1945 Pocket Books (A 2.2) edition notes 5 Grosset & Dunlap printings between July 1930 and September 1934.

A 2.1.f
Sixth printing: Dashiell Hammett Omnibus. New York: Knopf, 1935.

See AA 1.

Note: Copyright page notes that *The Dain Curse* has been '*Reprinted seven times*'.

A 2.1.g
Seventh printing: The Complete Dashiell Hammett. New York: Knopf, 1942.

See AA 1.c.

A 2.1.h
Eighth printing: New York: Grosset & Dunlap (Madison Square Books), 1943.

Not seen.

A 2.1.i
Ninth printing (1946)

[Black widow seal] | [decorated rule] | THE | Dain Curse | BY *Dashiell Hammett* | [decorated rule] | ALFRED A. KNOPF | NEW YORK.

Copyright page: '*First issued as a BLACK WIDOW THRILLER January 1946*'.

A 2.2.a
Second edition, first printing (1945)

[within shaded single-rule frame] *The* | DAIN | CURSE | *by* | *Dashiell Hammett* | [Pocket Books seal] | Pocket BOOKS, Inc. | New York, N.Y.

Copyright page: '*Pocket* BOOK *edition published May, 1945* | 1ST PRINTING [13 dots] MAY, 1945'.

#295.

Reprints noted: '2ND PRINTING [13 dots] MAY, 1945 | 3RD PRINTING [13 dots] JUNE, 1945'.

A 2.3
Third edition: The Dashiell Hammett Omnibus. London, Toronto, Melbourne, Sydney, Wellington: Cassell, 1950.

See AA 3.

A 2.4
Fourth edition (1959)

[vertical rule down center of page] A WDL BOOK | THE DAIN CURSE | Dashiell Hammett | WORLD DISTRIBUTORS • LONDON

#M718.

A 2.5
Fifth edition (1961)

[tapered vertical rule through center of page] DASHIELL | HAMMETT | THE DAIN | CURSE | [anchor device] PERMABOOKS • NEW YORK

Copyright page: 'PERMABOOK edition published March, 1961 | 1st printing [23 dots] January, 1961'.

#M4198.

A 2.6
Sixth edition: The Novels of Dashiell Hammett. New York: Knopf, 1965.

See AA 4.

A 2.7.a
Seventh edition, first printing (1966)

Dashiell Hammett | The Dain Curse | Penguin Books

Copyright page: 'Published in Penguin Books 1966'.

Harmondsworth. #C 2483.

Note: Copyright page states 'Published in Great Britain by Cassell 1931'. No Cassell publication of *The Dain Curse* has been located, and the likelihood is that Cassell simply distributed copies of the London Knopf printing. See A 4.1 for a similar case.

A 2.7.b
Seventh edition, second printing (1975)

Dashiell Hammett | The Dain Curse | Pan Books Ltd London and Sydney

Copyright page: 'This edition published 1975 by Pan Books Ltd'.

A 2.8
Eighth edition (1968)

The Dain Curse | [jagged rule] | DASHIELL HAMMETT | A DELL BOOK

Copyright page: 'First Dell Printing—April 1968'.

New York.

A 2.9
Ninth edition (1972)

The | *Dain Curse* | DASHIELL HAMMETT | [Vintage seal] | VINTAGE BOOKS | *A Division of Random House* | NEW YORK

Copyright page: 'Vintage Books Edition, October 1972'.

#V-287.

A 2.10
Tenth edition (1974)

Dashiell Hammett | THE DAIN CURSE | UNIFORM EDITION | [woman with bow] | CASSELL • LONDON

1974.

A 3 THE MALTESE FALCON

A 3.1.a
First edition, first printing (1930)

DASHIELL HAMMETT

THE MALTESE FALCON

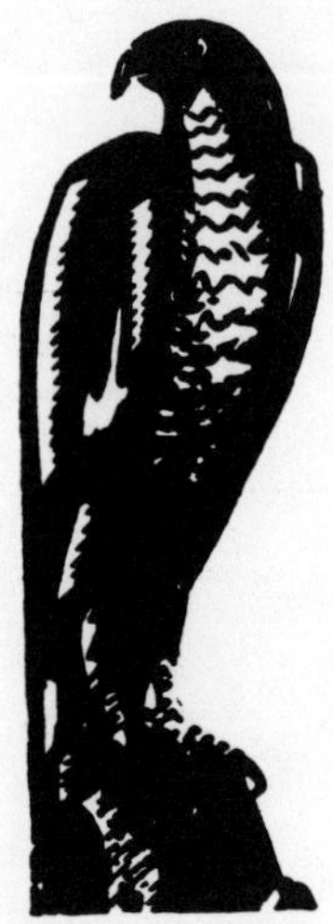

New York · ALFRED·A·KNOPF · *London*
1930

A 3.1.a: 7³/₈" × 5¹/₈"

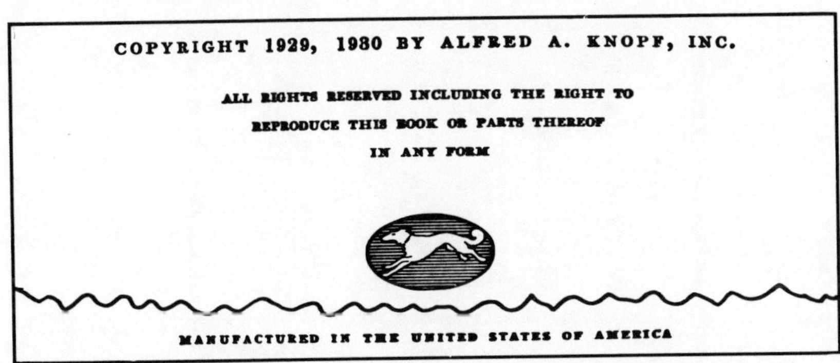

COPYRIGHT 1929, 1930 BY ALFRED A. KNOPF, INC.

ALL RIGHTS RESERVED INCLUDING THE RIGHT TO REPRODUCE THIS BOOK OR PARTS THEREOF IN ANY FORM

MANUFACTURED IN THE UNITED STATES OF AMERICA

$[1–17]^{8}$ $[18]^{6}$

[i–xii] [1–2] 3–267 [268–272]

Contents: pp. i–iv: blank; p. v: half title; p. vi: card page; p. vii: title; p. viii: copyright; p. ix: dedication; p. x: blank; pp. xi–xii: contents; p. 1: half title; p. 2: blank; pp. 3–267: text, headed 'CHAPTER I | *Spade & Archer';* p. 268: blurb and colophon; pp. 269–272: blank.

Typography and paper: 5 3/4" (6") × 3 11/16". 32 lines per page. Running heads: rectos, chapter titles; versos, 'THE MALTESE FALCON'. Wove paper.

Binding: Light gray V cloth (smooth). Front: dark grayish blue falcon within black single-rule frame. Spine: 5 blue and black decorated panels; '[in gray against black panel] THE | MALTESE | FALCON | DASHIELL | HAMMETT | [in blue against gray panel] KNOPF | NEW YORK'. Back: stamped black rectangle outlining Borzoi seal in lower right-hand corner. White wove sized endpapers. Top and bottom edges trimmed. Top edge stained blue.

Dust jacket: Front: '[drawing against blue background of falcon and hand holding coins and jewelry rising from water] THE | MALTESE | FALCON | BY | DASHIELL | HAMMETT | AUTHOR OF | THE DAIN CURSE'. Spine: 'THE | MALTESE | FALCON | BY | DASHIELL | HAMMETT | [drawing of falcon] | ALFRED A. | KNOPF | [Borzoi seal within single-rule frame]'. Back: 'By DASHIELL HAMMETT | RED HARVEST | [8 lines of blurbs by Herbert Asbury and *The Outlook*] | $2.00 | THE DAIN CURSE | [11 lines of blurbs by Will Cuppy and Walter Brooks] | $2.00 | ALFRED A. KNOPF [Borzoi seal] PUBLISHER, N. Y.' Front flap: '$2.00 | THE | MALTESE FALCON | BY | DASHIELL HAMMETT | [description of book]'. Back flap: 'DASHIELL HAMMETT | [continuation of description of book and biographical information about Hammett]'.

Publication: Unknown number of copies of the first printing. $2.00. Published 14 February 1930. Copyright 14 February 1930. Copyright #A18946.

Printing: Plates, printing, and binding by Vail-Ballou.

Note: *The Maltese Falcon* was first published in *Black Mask* in 5 parts; see C 109.

Locations: BL ('31 MAR 30'); Bod ('Dec 2 1930'); InU; OKentC (dj); RL.

A 3.1.b–f
Second through sixth printings (1930)

Not seen.

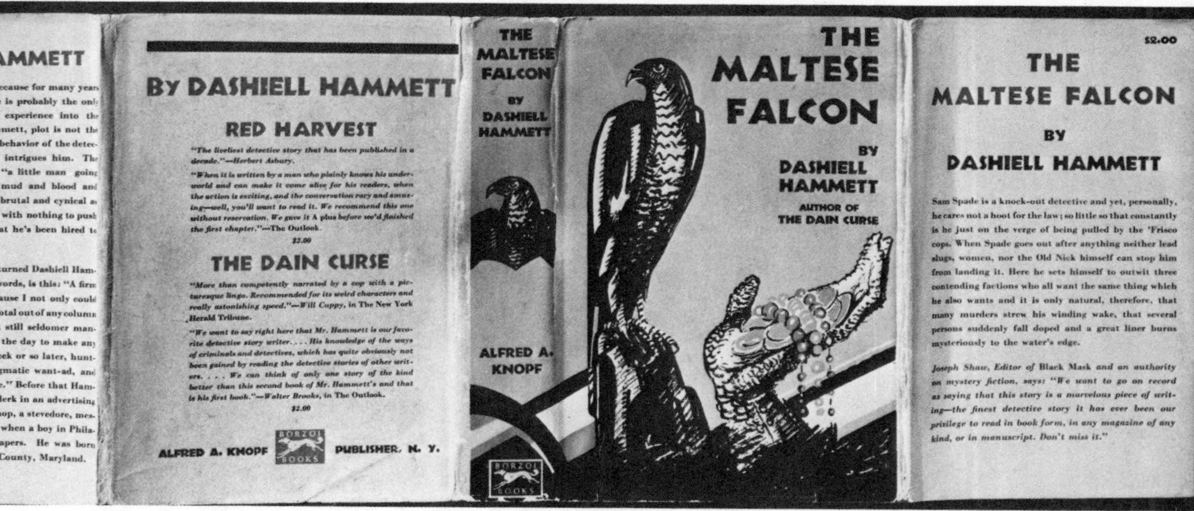

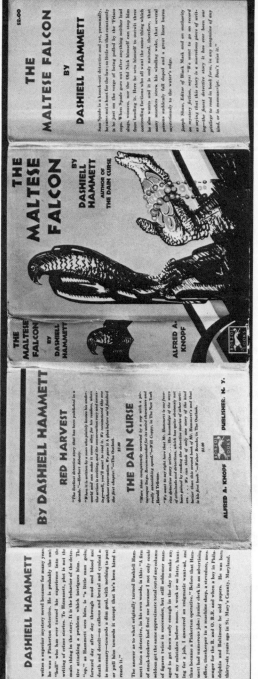

Dust jacket for A 3.1.a

A 3.1.g
Seventh printing (1930)

THE MALTESE | FALCON | BY | DASHIELL HAMMETT | AUTHOR OF | THE DAIN CURSE, | RED HARVEST, Etc. | [device] | GROSSET & DUNLAP | PUBLISHERS NEW YORK

Copyright page: 'PUBLISHED FEBRUARY 1930 | SECOND PRINTING, MARCH, 1930 | THIRD PRINTING, APRIL, 1930 | FOURTH PRINTING, JUNE, 1930 | FIFTH PRINTING, SEPTEMBER, 1930 | SIXTH PRINTING, NOVEMBER, 1930'.

A 3.1.h
Eighth printing (1934)

[within double-rules frame] THE | MALTESE | FALCON | [rule] | BY | DASHİELL HAMMETT | [rule] | WITH A NEW INTRODUCTION | BY THE AUTHOR | [rule] | [Modern Library seal] | [rule] | BENNETT A. CERF • DONALD S. KLOPFER | THE MODERN LIBRARY | NEW YORK

Copyright page: 'First Modern Library Edition | 1934'.

A 3.1.i
Ninth printing (1934?)

[within single-rule frame with running figure at top] THE | MALTESE | FALCON | BY | DASHIELL | HAMMETT | WITH A NEW INTRODUCTION | BY THE AUTHOR | [outside frame] MODERN LIBRARY • NEW YORK

1934?

A 3.1.j
Tenth printing: Toronto: Macmillan, 1934.

Not seen.

A 3.1.k
Eleventh printing: Dashiell Hammett Omnibus. New York: Knopf, 1935.

See AA 1.

Note: Copyright page notes that *The Maltese Falcon* has been *'Reprinted thirteen times'.*

A 3.1.l
Twelfth printing: The Complete Dashiell Hammett. New York: Knopf, 1942.

See AA 1.c.

A 3.1.m
Thirteenth printing (1943)

THE MALTESE | FALCON | BY DASHIELL HAMMETT | [6-line notice that book was produced under wartime conditions, bordered on either side by decorative device] | [device] | GROSSET & DUNLAP | PUBLISHERS

1943. New York.

A 3.1.n
Fourteenth printing (1943)

THE | MALTESE FALCON | *By* | *Dashiell Hammett* | [drawing of boy] | ZEPHYR | BOOKS | The Continental Book Company AB | STOCKHOLM

1943. #19.

A 3.1.o
Fifteenth printing (1945)

[following 3 lines within 2 double-line ovals] A BLACK | WIDOW | [drawing of spider] | THRILLER | [decorated rule] | THE | Maltese Falcon | BY *Dashiell Hammett* | [decorated rule] | ALFRED • A • KNOPF | NEW YORK

Copyright page: 'Published February 1930 | First issued as a BLACK WIDOW THRILLER January 1945'.

A 3.2
Second edition, first English printing (1930)

DASHIELL HAMMETT

THE MALTESE FALCON

London · ALFRED · A · KNOPF · *New York*
1930

A 3.2: 7 3/8″ × 4 13/16″

PRINTED IN ENGLAND FOR
ALFRED A. KNOPF LIMITED
BY RICHARD CLAY AND SONS,
LTD., BUNGAY, SUFFOLK.

[A] B–I K–R^8 S^4

[1–10] 11–280

Contents: p.1: half title; p. 2: card page; p. 3: title; p. 4: copyright; p. 5: dedication; p. 6: blank; p. 7: 'CONTENTS'; p. 8: blank; p. 9: half title; p. 10: blank; pp. 11–280: text, headed 'CHAPTER I | SPADE AND ARCHER'.

Typography and paper: $5^{5}/_{16}$″ ($5^{1}/_{2}$″) × $3^{7}/_{16}$″. 32 lines per page. Running heads: rectos, chapter titles; versos, 'THE MALTESE FALCON'. Laid paper.

Binding: Bright blue shellacked V cloth. Front: Falcon stamped in black in upper right-hand corner. Spine: '[black decorated rule] | [in red] THE | MALTESE | FALCON | DASHIELL | HAMMETT | [black falcon] | [in red] KNOPF | [black decorated rule]'. Back: stamped black rectangle outlining Borzoi seal in lower right-hand corner. Sized endpapers. All edges trimmed. Top edge stained blue.

Dust jacket: Not seen.

Publication: Published July 1930. 7s. 6d.

Printing: Printed in England by Richard Clay and Sons.

Location: RL.

A 3.3.a
Third edition, first printing (1944)

[within shaded frame] *The* | MALTESE | FALCON | BY | DASHIELL HAMMETT | POCKET ['BOOKS' in hollow letters] BOOKS INC. [kangaroo] NEW YORK, 20 N.Y.

Copyright page: '1ST PRINTING [11 dots] JULY, 1944'.

Typography: On verso of front free endpaper: 'AUGUST, 1944 | Pocket BOOK BEST SELLERS | [list of titles and numbers, beginning with *Lost Horizon,* ending with *The Thin Man*]'; continued on recto of rear free endpaper, beginning with *The Pocket Book of War Humor,* ending with *Here Is Your War.*

#268.

Reprints noted: (1) '4TH PRINTING [5 dots] FEBRUARY, 1945'. Published with dust jacket over wrappers. Front cover illustration by Stanley Mettyoff is same as first printing. (2) '8TH PRINTING [5 dots] OCTOBER, 1945'. First 60 pages on different stock than remaining pages. "Perma-Gloss" binding.

A 3.4
Fourth edition, first printing (1944)

DASHIELL HAMMETT'S | MYSTERY OMNIBUS CONTAINING TWO COMPLETE AND UNABRIDGED NOVELS | THE MALTESE FALCON and THE GLASS KEY | [Forum Books seal] CLEVELAND THE WORLD PUBLISHING COMPANY NEW YORK

Copyright page: 'FORUM BOOKS EDITION | *First Printing August 1944* | [14 lines on books in wartime] | HC [H is badly damaged]'.

A 3.5
Fifth edition: The Dashiell Hammett Omnibus. London, Toronto, Melbourne, Sydney, Wellington: Cassell, 1950.

See AA 3.

A 3.6
Sixth edition: London: Pan Books, 1952.

Not seen.

A 3.7.a
Seventh edition, first printing (1957)

• | THE | MALTESE | FALCON | • | BY DASHIELL HAMMETT | [anchor device] | PERMABOOKS • NEW YORK

Copyright page: '1st printing [27 dots] January, 1957'.

#M3074.

A 3.7.b
Seventh edition, second printing (1961)

DASHIELL | HAMMETT | THE | ['M' in reverse printing over black falcon] MALTESE | FALCON | [rule interrupted by 'FALCON'] | [anchor device] PERMABOOKS • NEW YORK

Copyright page: '2nd printing [23 dots] January 1961'.

#M4200.

A 3.8
Eighth edition: London: Hamilton, 1958.

Not seen.

A 3.9.a
Ninth edition, first printing (1963)

The Maltese Falcon | [tapered rule] | DASHIELL HAMMETT | PENGUIN BOOKS

Copyright page: 'Published in Penguin Books 1963'.

1963. Harmondsworth. #1887.

A 3.9.b
Ninth edition, second printing: Harmondsworth: Penguin, 1966.

Copyright page: 'Reprinted 1966'.

A 3.9.c
Ninth edition, third printing (1975)

Dashiell Hammett | The Maltese falcon | Pan Books Ltd London and Sydney

Copyright page: 'This edition published 1975'.

A 3.10.a
Tenth edition, first printing (1964)

[device] | THE Maltese Falcon | & | The | Thin Man | BY | DASHIELL HAMMETT | [Vintage seal] | VINTAGE BOOKS | *A Division of Random House* | NEW YORK

Copyright page: 'VINTAGE EDITION, *March, 1964*'.

#V-255.

Reprint noted: Title page: 'The | Maltese | Falcon | DASHIELL HAMMETT | [Vintage seal] | VINTAGE BOOKS | *A Division of Random House* | NEW YORK'. Copyright page: 'Vintage Books Edition, May 1972'. #V-772.

A 3.11
Eleventh edition: The Novels of Dashiell Hammett. New York: Knopf, 1965.

See AA 4.

A 3.12
Twelfth edition (1966)

[all within single-rule frame] [within another single-rule frame] DASHIELL | HAMMETT | [within another single-rule frame, against black background] THE | MALTESE | FALCON | [within another single-rule frame, against white background] A DELL BOOK

Copyright page: 'First Dell Printing—July, 1966'.

New York. #5175

A 3.13
Thirteenth edition (1974)

Dashiell Hammett | THE MALTESE FALCON | UNIFORM EDITION | [woman with bow] | CASSELL • LONDON

Copyright page: 'First published in this edition 1974'.

A 3.14
Fourteenth (?) edition

THE | MALTESE | FALCON | DASHIELL HAMMETT | ALFRED • A • KNOPF | NEW YORK

Mystery Guild Book Club edition. Date not established.

A 3.15
Fifteenth edition (1972)

The | *Maltese* | *Falcon* | DASHIELL HAMMETT | [Vintage seal] | VINTAGE BOOKS | A Division of Random House | New York

Copyright page: 'Vintage Books Edition, May 1972'.

Foot of p. 229: '2–76'.

#V-772.

A 3.16

Sixteenth edition: *The Maltese Falcon Large Print Edition.* Bath: Cedric Cheevers, 1977.

Note

In 1946 King Features published a comic-book version of *The Maltese Falcon* illustrated by Rodlow Willard. Feature Book #48.

A 4 THE GLASS KEY

A 4.1
First English edition (1931)

DASHIELL HAMMETT

THE
GLASS KEY

London · ALFRED · A · KNOPF · *New York*
1931

A 4.1: 7 3/8" × 4 7/8"

PRINTED IN ENGLAND FOR
ALFRED A. KNOPF LIMITED
BY RICHARD CLAY AND SONS,
LTD., BUNGAY, SUFFOLK.

[A] B–I K–S^8

[1–10] 11–285 [286–288]

Contents: p. 1: half title; p. 2: card page; p. 3: title; p. 4: copyright; p. 5: dedication; p. 6: blank; p. 7: 'CONTENTS'; p. 8: blank; p. 9: half title; p. 10: blank; pp. 11–285: text, headed 'CHAPTER I | THE BODY IN CHINA STREET | I'; pp. 286–288: blank.

Typography and paper: 5^5/$_{16}$" (5^1/$_2$") × 3^1/$_4$". 32 lines per page. Running heads: rectos, chapter titles; versos, 'THE GLASS KEY'. Laid paper.

Binding: Blue V cloth. Front: white key in upper right-hand corner. Spine: '[stamped in red] [decorated rule] | THE | GLASS | KEY | DASHIELL | HAMMETT | [white key] | [red] KNOPF | [decorated rule]'. Back: rectangular Borzoi seal in lower right-hand corner. Wove endpapers. All edges trimmed. Top edge stained blue.

Also noted bound as follows: Blue shellacked V cloth (smooth). Front: stamped reddish orange key in upper right-hand corner. Spine: '[stamped in reddish orange] [decorated rule] | THE | GLASS | KEY | DASHIELL | HAMMETT | [vertical key] | CASSELL | [decorated rule]'. Back: blank. Wove endpapers. All edges trimmed. Top edge stained blue.

Dust jacket: Not seen.

Publication: Published 20 January 1931 (according to copyright application). 7s. 6d.

Printing: Printed in England by Richard Clay and Sons.

Note: *The Glass Key* was first published in *Black Mask* in 4 parts; see C 115–C 118.

Locations: BL ('8 JAN 1931', Knopf binding); Bod ('JUN 6 1931', Cassell binding); LC ('MAR 19 1931', rebound); RL (Cassell binding).

A 4.2.a
Second edition, first American printing (1931)

DASHIELL HAMMETT

THE GLASS KEY

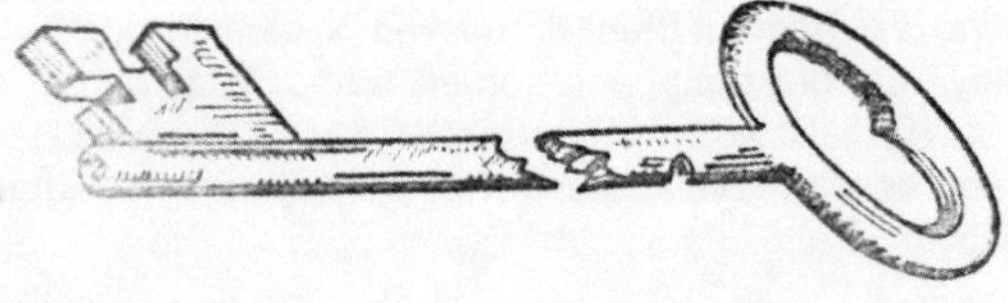

New York · ALFRED · A · KNOPF · *London*
1 9 3 1

A 4.2.a: $7^{3}/_{8}'' \times 5^{1}/_{8}''$

Manufactured in the United States of America

[1–17][8] [18][10]

[i–viii] [1–2] 3–282 [283–284]

Contents: p. i: half title; p. ii: card page; p. iii: title; p. iv: copyright; p. v: dedication; p. vi: blank; p. vii: *'CONTENTS';* p. viii: blank; p. 1: half title; p. 2: blank; pp. 3–282: text, headed 'CHAPTER I | *The Body in China Street* | i'; p. 283: blank; p. 284: colophon.

Typography and paper: 5$^3/_8$" (5$^9/_{16}$") × 3$^1/_2$". 29 or 30 lines per page. Running heads: rectos, chapter titles; versos, 'THE GLASS KEY'. Wove paper.

Binding: Light green V cloth (smooth). Front: stamped dark green broken key within stamped red single-rule frame. Spine: 5 panels with stamped decorations in dark green and red; '[in light green against red panel] THE | GLASS | KEY | DASHIELL | HAMMETT | [in dark green against light green panel] KNOPF | NEW YORK'. Back: Borzoi seal outlined against dark green stamped panel in lower right-hand corner. White wove sized endpapers. All edges trimmed. Top edge stained burgundy.

Dust jacket: Front: '[photograph of woman's face outlined by handcuff against green background] the | GLASS | KEY | DASHIELL HAMMETT | AUTHOR OF THE MALTESE FALCON'. Spine: '[vertical drawing of broken key interrupted by title and author's name] [rule] | THE | GLASS KEY | [short rule] | DASHIELL | HAMMETT | [rule] | [Borzoi seal] | ALFRED A. | KNOPF'. Back: same as front. Front flap: 'THE | GLASS | KEY | *by Dashiell Hammett* | *author of the Maltese Falcon* | [description of book] | *(Jacket photograph reproduced through the* | *courtesy of Paramount Pictures)*'. Back flap: 'THE DETECTIVE | STORIES OF | *Dashiell Hammett* | [6 lines of type and blurbs for *The Maltese Falcon, The Dain Curse,* and *Red Harvest*]'.

Publication: Unknown number of copies of the first printing. $2.50. Published 24 April 1931. Copyright 24 April 1931. Copyright #A36854.

Note: Publication price was $2.50. A Knopf ad in the 23 May 1931 issue of *Publishers Weekly* announced a decrease to $2.00, with a return to the price of $2.50 after 1 June 1931.

Printing: Plates, printing, and binding by Vail-Ballou, Binghamton, N.Y.

Locations: DLC ('MAR 19 1931', rebound); OKentC (dj); RL.

A 4.2.b–e
Second edition, second through fifth printings (1931)

Reprints noted: (1) Copyright page: '*Published April, 1931* | *First and second print-*

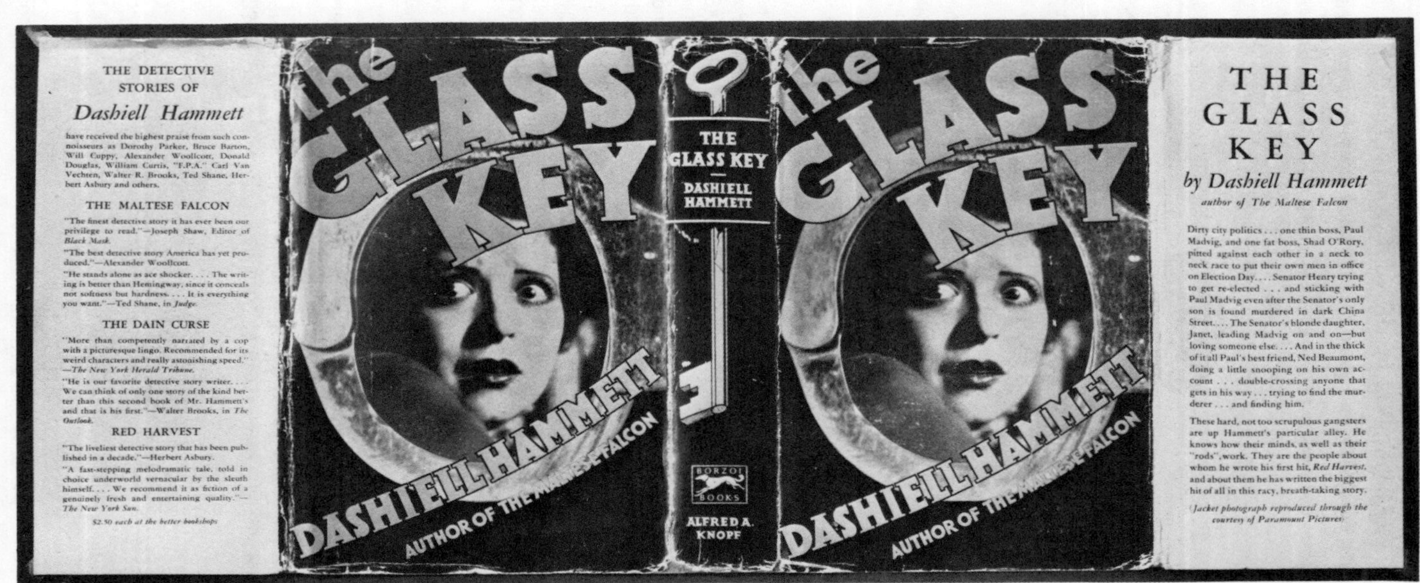

Dust jacket for A 4.2.a

ings before publication'. LC deposit stamp: 'APR 30 1931'. (2) Copyright page: *'Published April, 1931 | First, second and third printings | before publication'.* (3) Copyright page: *'Published April, 1931 | First, second and third printings | before publication | Fourth printing May 1931 | Fifth printing May 1931'.*

Note: *Publishers Weekly*, 16 December 1933, stated: "Over 20,000 copies of *The Glass Key* have been sold at $2.50 at this date."

A 4.2.f
Second edition, sixth printing (1933)

DASHIELL HAMMETT | [wavy rule] | THE GLASS | KEY | [drawing of broken key] | [wavy rule] | GROSSET & DUNLAP | *Publishers New York*

Copyright page: *'. . . Fifth printing May 1931'.*

1933.

Note: Copyright page of 1943 Pocket Books edition (A 4.4) notes 4 Grosset & Dunlap printings between November 1933 and May 1939.

A 4.2.g
Second edition, seventh printing: New York: Grosset & Dunlap, 1942.

Not seen.

A 4.2.h
Second edition, eighth printing: The Complete Dashiell Hammett. New York: Knopf, 1942.

See AA 1.c.

Note: Pocket Books edition (A 4.4.a) notes 2 printings.

A 4.3
Third edition: Cleveland: World, 1939.

Not seen.

A 4.4.a
Fourth edition, first printing (1943)

[within shaded-rules frame, with 5 rules on left and bottom, 7 rules on top and right] THE | GLASS KEY | *DASHIELL HAMMETT* | ['pb' in reverse printing on black circle] | POCKET ['BOOKS' in hollow letters] BOOKS INC. | New York

Copyright page: *'Pocket* BOOKS *edition published April, 1943* | 1ST PRINTING [5 dots] FEBRUARY, 1943'.

#211.

Reprints noted: (1) '4TH PRINTING [5 dots] SEPTEMBER, 1943'. (2) '9TH PRINTING [5 dots] NOVEMBER, 1945'.

A 4.5
Fifth edition (1944)

DASHIELL HAMMETT'S | MYSTERY OMNIBUS CONTAINING TWO COMPLETE AND UNABRIDGED NOVELS | THE MALTESE FALCON and THE GLASS KEY | [Forum Books seal] CLEVELAND THE WORLD PUBLISHING COMPANY NEW YORK

Copyright page: 'FORUM BOOKS EDITION | *First Printing August 1944* [14 lines on books in wartime] HC [H is badly damaged]'.

A 4.6
Sixth edition: New York: Knopf, 1945.

Not seen.

A 4.7
Seventh edition: Cleveland: World, 1946.

Not seen.

A 4.8
Eighth edition: The Dashiell Hammett Omnibus. London, Toronto, Melbourne, Sydney, Wellington: Cassell, 1950.

See AA 3.

A 4.9.a
Ninth edition, first printing: London: Brown, Watson, 1957.

A Digit Book. Not seen.

Reprint noted: London: Brown, Watson, 1958. Not seen.

A 4.10
Tenth edition (1961)

[page divided by vertical decorated rule] [left of rule] DASHIELL HAMMETT | [anchor device] | PERMABOOKS • NEW YORK | [right of rule] The | Glass | Key

Copyright page: 'PERMABOOK edition published March, 1961 | 1st printing [23 dots] January, 1961'.

#M 4199.

A 4.11
Eleventh edition: The Novels of Dashiell Hammett. New York: Knopf, 1965.

See AA 4.

A 4.12
Twelfth edition (1966)

[all within single-rule frame] [within another single-rule frame] DASHIELL | HAMMETT | [within another single-rule frame, in reverse printing against black background] THE | GLASS | KEY | [within another single-rule frame] A DELL BOOK

Copyright page: 'First Dell Printing—July, 1966'.

New York. #2915.

A 4.13.a
Thirteenth edition, first printing (1966)

Dashiell Hammett | The Glass Key | [Penguin seal] Penguin Books

Copyright page: 'Published in Penguin Books 1966'.

Harmondsworth. #C 2435.

A 4.13.b
Thirteenth edition, second printing: London: Pan Books, 1975.

Not seen.

A 4.13.c
Thirteenth edition, third printing (1975)

Dashiell Hammett | The Glass Key | Pan Books London and Sydney

Copyright page: 'This edition published 1975 by Pan Books Ltd, | Cavaye Place, London SW 10 9PG | 2nd Printing 1977'.

A 4.14
Fourteenth edition (1972)

The | *Glass Key* | DASHIELL HAMMETT | [Vintage seal] VINTAGE BOOKS | *A Division of Random House* | NEW YORK

Copyright page: 'Vintage books edition, May 1972'.

A 4.15
Fifteenth edition (1974)

Dashiell Hammett | THE GLASS KEY | UNIFORM EDITION | [Woman with bow] | Cassell • London

1974.

A 5 CREEPS BY NIGHT

A 5.1.a
First edition, first printing (1931)

CREEPS
BY
NIGHT

CHILLS AND THRILLS

SELECTED BY

DASHIELL HAMMETT

•0•

THE JOHN DAY COMPANY

NEW YORK

A 5.1.a: 7³/₈″ × 5¹/₈″

INTRODUCTION, Copyright, 1931, by Dashiell Hammett.

A ROSE FOR EMILY, Copyright, 1930, by The Forum.

GREEN THOUGHTS, Copyright, 1931, by Harper & Brothers.

THE GHOST OF ALEXANDER PERKS, A.B., Copyright, 1931, by The Atlantic Monthly Co.

THE HOUSE, Copyright, 1931, by Harper & Brothers.

THE KILL, Copyright, 1931, by Peter Fleming.

TEN O'CLOCK, Copyright, 1931, by Philip MacDonald.

THE SPIDER, Copyright, 1931, by The John Day Co.

BREAKDOWN, Copyright, 1929, by The Forum.

THE WITCH'S VENGEANCE, Copyright, 1930, by the International Magazine Co.

THE RAT, Copyright, 1929, by the Popular Fiction Co.

FAITH, HOPE AND CHARITY, Copyright, 1930, by the International Magazine Co.

MR. ARCULARIS, Copyright, 1931, by Harper & Brothers.

THE MUSIC OF ERICH ZANN, Copyright, 1925, by the Popular Fiction Co.

The STRANGE CASE OF MRS. ARKWRIGHT, Copyright, 1928, by the International Magazine Co.

THE KING OF THE CATS, Copyright, 1929, by Stephen Vincent Benet.

THE RED BRAIN, Copyright, 1927, by the Popular Fiction Co.

THE PHANTOM BUS, Copyright, 1930, by the Popular Fiction Co.

BEYOND THE DOOR, Copyright, 1930, by the Popular Fiction Co.

PERCHANCE TO DREAM, Copyright, 1931, by Michael Joyce.

A VISITOR FROM EGYPT, Copyright, 1930, by the Popular Fiction Co.

$[1–16]^{16}$ $[17]^{8}$

[i–ii] [1–4] 5–9 [10–12] 15–63 [64] 65–85 [86] 87–141 [142] 143–185 [186] 187–209 [210] 211–271 [272] 273–309 [310] 311–363 [364] 365–393 [394] 395–439 [440] 441–481 [482] 483–503 [504] 505–525 [526–528]

Contents: pp. i–ii: blank; p. 1: half title; p. 2: blank; p. 3: title; p.4: copyright; pp. 5–6: contents; pp. 7–9: introduction; p. 10: blank; p. 11: half title; p. 12: blank; no pp. 13–14, pp. 15–525, text, headed 'A ROSE FOR EMILY | *By* | *William Faulkner* | [tapered rule]'; pp. 526–528: blank.

20 stories: "Introduction," Hammett; "A Rose for Emily," William Faulkner; "Green Thoughts," John Collier; "The Ghost of Alexander Perks, A.B.," Robert Dean Frisbie; "The House," André Maurois; "The Kill," Peter Fleming; "Ten O'Clock," Philip MacDonald; "The Spider," Hanns Heinz Ewers; "Breakdown," L. A. G. Strong; "The Witch's Vengeance," W. B. Seabrook; "The Rat," S. Fowler Wright; "Faith, Hope and Charity," Irvin S. Cobb; "Mr. Arcularis," Conrad Aiken; "The Music of Erich Zann," H. P. Lovecraft; "The Strange Case of Mrs. Arkwright," Harold Dearden; "The King of the Cats," Stephen Vincent Benét; "The Red Brain," Donald Wandrei; "The Phantom Bus," W. Elwyn Backus; "Beyond the Door," Paul Suter; "Perchance to Dream," Michael Joyce; "A Visitor from Egypt," Frank Belknap Long, Jr.

Typography and paper: 5¼″ (5¹¹⁄₁₆″) × 3½″. 27 lines per page. Running heads: rectos, story titles; versos, 'CREEPS BY NIGHT'. Wove paper.

Binding: Black V cloth (smooth). Front: '[stamped in green] [3 vertical wavy lines] | [printed vertically] CREEPS BY NIGHT'. Spine: '[stamped in green] [wavy rule] | CREEPS | BY | NIGHT | [2 wavy rules] | DASHIELL HAMMETT | [2 wavy rules] | JOHN DAY | [wavy rule]'. Back: blank. Green sized endpapers. Top and botton edges trimmed. Top edge stained green.

Dust jacket: Not seen.

Publication: Unknown number of copies of the first printing. $2.50. Published 8 October 1931. Copyright 23 September 1931. Copyright #A45044–A45048.

Printing: Plates, printing, and binding by J. J. Little & Ives.

Locations: LC; NcU; RL.

A 5.1.b
Second printing (1932)

CREEPS | BY | NIGHT | CHILLS AND THRILLS | SELECTED BY | DASHIELL HAMMETT | • O • | TUDOR PUBLISHING CO. | NEW YORK

Copyright page: '*SECOND PRINTING, JANUARY, 1932*'.

A 5.1.c
Third printing (1936)

CREEPS | BY | NIGHT | CHILLS AND THRILLS | SELECTED BY | DASHIELL HAMMETT | [within circle over drawing of open book] brb | BLUE RIBBON BOOKS, INC. | NEW YORK CITY

1936.

A 5.1.d
Fourth printing (1944)

CREEPS | BY NIGHT | CHILLS AND THRILLS | SELECTED BY | DASHIELL HAMMETT | [rule interrupted by Forum seal] | THE WORLD PUBLISHING COMPANY | CLEVELAND AND NEW YORK

Copyright page: 'FORUM BOOKS EDITION | *First Printing January 1944*'.

A 5.2.a
Second edition, first English printing (1932)

MODERN
TALES OF HORROR

selected by
DASHIELL HAMMETT

LONDON
VICTOR GOLLANCZ LTD
14 Henrietta Street Covent Garden
1932

A 5.2.a: 7⅝" × 5¼"

Copyright page: 'Printed in Great Britain by | The Camelot Press Ltd., London and Southampton | *on paper supplied by* Spalding & Hodge Ltd. | *and bound by* | The Leighton-Straker Bookbinding Co. Ltd.'.

[AH] BH–IH KH–UH WH–ZH AAH–DDH^8

[1–4] 5 [6] 7–10 [11–12] 13–61 [62] 63–83 [84] 85–139 [140] 141–183 [184] 185–227 [228] 229–299 [300] 301–317 [318] 319–375 [376] 377–405 [406] 407–427 [428] 429–448

Contents: p.1: half title; p. 2: blank; p. 3: title; p. 4: copyright; p. 5: contents; p. 6: blank; pp. 7–10: introduction by Hammett; p. 11: half title; p. 12: blank; pp. 13–448: text, headed 'A ROSE FOR EMILY | *By* | *William Faulkner* | I'.

18 stories: Omits "The Rat" and "The Strange Case of Mrs. Arkwright."

Typography and paper: 5$^{13}/_{16}$" (5$^3/_8$") × 3$^5/_8$". 27 lines per page. Running heads: rectos, story titles; versos, 'MODERN TALES OF HORROR'. Wove paper.

Binding: Black V cloth (smooth). Front: blank. Spine: '[printed in orange] MODERN | TALES OF | HORROR | GOLLANCZ'. Back: blank.

Dust Jacket: not seen.

Publication: Unknown number of copies of the first printing. 5s.

Printing: Printing by The Camelot Press Ltd., London and Southampton; binding by The Leighton-Straker Bookbinding Co. Ltd.

Location: RL.

Note: Tipped-in label on free front endpaper reads as follows: 'John Collier's story GREEN THOUGHTS was | published in a limited edition by Messrs. | Joiner & Steele in February, 1932, and is here | reproduced by their courteous permission.'

A 5.2.b
Second edition, second printing (1932)

Copyright page: '*First published July 1932* | *Second impression July 1932*'.

A 5.3
Third edition (1961)

CREEPS | BY NIGHT | Selected and with a special introduction by | DASHIELL HAMMETT | [Belmont Books seal]

Copyright page: 'BELMONT BOOKS Edition 1961'.

Contents: "Introduction," Dashiell Hammett; "A Rose for Emily," William Faulkner; "The House," André Maurois; "The Spider," Hanns Heinz Ewers; "The Witch's Vengeance," W. B. Seabrook; "Mr. Arcularis," Conrad Aiken; "The Strange Case of Mrs. Arkwright," Harold Dearden; "The King of the Cats," Stephen Vincent Benét; "Beyond the Door," Paul Suter; "Perchance to Dream," Michael Joyce; "A Visitor from Egypt," Frank Belknap Long, Jr.

#230.

A 5.4
Fourth edition (1961)

THE | RED | BRAIN | And other thrillers | Selected and with a | special introduction by | DASHIELL HAMMETT | from Creeps by Night | [Belmont Books seal]

Copyright page: 'BELMONT BOOKS Edition 1961'.

Contents: "Introduction," Dashiell Hammett; "Green Thoughts," John Collier; "The Ghost of Alexander Perks, A.B.," Robert Dean Frisbie; "The Kill," Peter Fleming; "Ten O'Clock," Philip MacDonald; "Breakdown," L. A. G. Strong; "The Rat," S. Fowler Wright; "Faith, Hope and Charity," Irvin S. Cobb; "The Music of Erich Zann," H. P. Lovecraft; "The Red Brain," Donald Wandrei; "The Phantom Bus," W. Elwyn Backus.

#239.

A 5.5
Fifth edition (1965)

The Red Brain | And other thrillers | Selected and with a special introduction by | DASHIELL HAMMETT | [in reverse printing against black square] 4 | A FOUR SQUARE BOOK

Copyright page: 'FIRST FOUR SQUARE EDITION September 1965'.

Contents same as A 5.4.

#1328.

A 5.6
Sixth edition (1966)

Creeps By Night | Ten Great Weird Tales | by Masters of the Horror Story | Selected and with a special | introduction by | DASHIELL HAMMETT | [in reverse printing against black square] 4 | A FOUR SQUARE BOOK

Copyright page: 'FIRST FOUR SQUARE EDITION February 1966'.

Contents same as A 5.3.

#1438.

A 5.7
Seventh edition (1968)

Breakdown | and other thrillers | Selected and with a special introduction by | DASHIELL HAMMETT | [within single-rule frame divided into thirds by vertical rules, each letter in a separate third] NEL | THE NEW ENGLISH LIBRARY

Copyright page: 'FIRST NEL EDITION JANUARY 1968'.

10 stories from *Creeps by Night.*

#1784.

A6 THE THIN MAN

A6.1.a
First edition, first printing (1934)

DASHIELL HAMMETT

THE

THIN MAN

New York 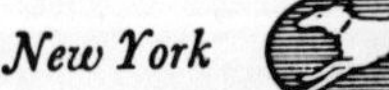  *Mcmxxxiv*

ALFRED · A · KNOPF

A6.1.a: 7 7/16" × 5 1/8"

Copyright 1934 by Alfred A. Knopf, Inc.

All rights reserved. No part of this book may be reproduced in any form without permission in writing from the publisher, except by a reviewer who may quote brief passages in a review to be printed in a magazine or newspaper.

First Edition

Manufactured in the United States of America

[1–17][8]

[i–x] [1–2] 3–258 [259–262]

Contents: pp. i–iii: blank; p. iv: card page with quote by Dorothy Parker; p. v: half title; p. vi: blank; p. vii: title; p. viii: copyright, '*First Edition*'; p. ix: dedication; p. x: blank; p. 1: half title; p. 2: blank; pp. 3–259: text, headed '[swash caps] *The Thin Man* | [rule] | *1*'; p. 260: colophon; pp. 261–262: blank.

Typography and paper: 5$^{9}/_{16}$" (6$^{1}/_{16}$") × 3$^{11}/_{16}$". 28 or 29 lines per page. Running heads: rectos and versos, 'THE THIN MAN | [rule]'. Wove paper.

Binding: Grayish yellow green V cloth (smooth). Front: stamped deep blue mask within stamped deep red frame. Spine: 5 panels with stamped decorations in red and blue; '[in yellow green against red panel] THE | THIN | MAN | DASHIELL | HAMMETT | [in dark blue against green panel] ALFRED • A • | KNOPF'. Back: stamped red rectangle outlining Borzoi seal in lower right-hand corner. White wove sized endpapers. All edges trimmed. Top edge stained burgundy.

Dust jacket: Front: '[photograph of Hammett holding cane] [vertically, beginning at bottom, on left of page] THE-THIN-MAN | [horizontally at bottom of page] DASHIELL | HAMMETT'. Spine: 'DASHIELL | HAMMETT | [rule] | THE | THIN | MAN | [photograph of Hammett holding cane] | [Borzoi seal] | ALFRED • A • | KNOPF'. Back: 'THE DETECTIVE STORIES OF | DASHIELL HAMMETT | [5 lines of type followed by blurbs for *The Glass Key, The Maltese Falcon, The Dain Curse,* and *Red Harvest*] | ALFRED • A • KNOPF [Borzoi seal] PUBLISHER, N. Y.'. Front flap: '$2.00 | net. | [description of book]'. Back flap: 'DASHIELL HAMMETT | [thick rule] | [biographical information about Hammett]'. Jacket noted with highlights in either red or green.

Publication: Unknown number of copies of the first printing. $2.00. Published 8 January 1934. Copyright 8 January 1934. Copyright #A67913.

Printing: Plates, printing, and binding by H. Wolff Estate.

Note 1: *Publishers Weekly,* 29 June 1935, indicates that *The Thin Man* sold 33,836 copies at $2.00.

Note 2: *The Thin Man* first appeared in *Redbook;* see C 128.

Locations: InU; OKentC (both red and green djs); RL.

A 6.1.b–f
Second through sixth printings (1934)

Reprints noted: (1) 'First and Second Printings Before Publication | Published January 8, 1934'. LC deposit stamp: 'JAN –9 1934' (2) '. . . Sixth Printing March, 1934'.

Note: A correction was made in the sixth printing: 209.17 seep [sleep

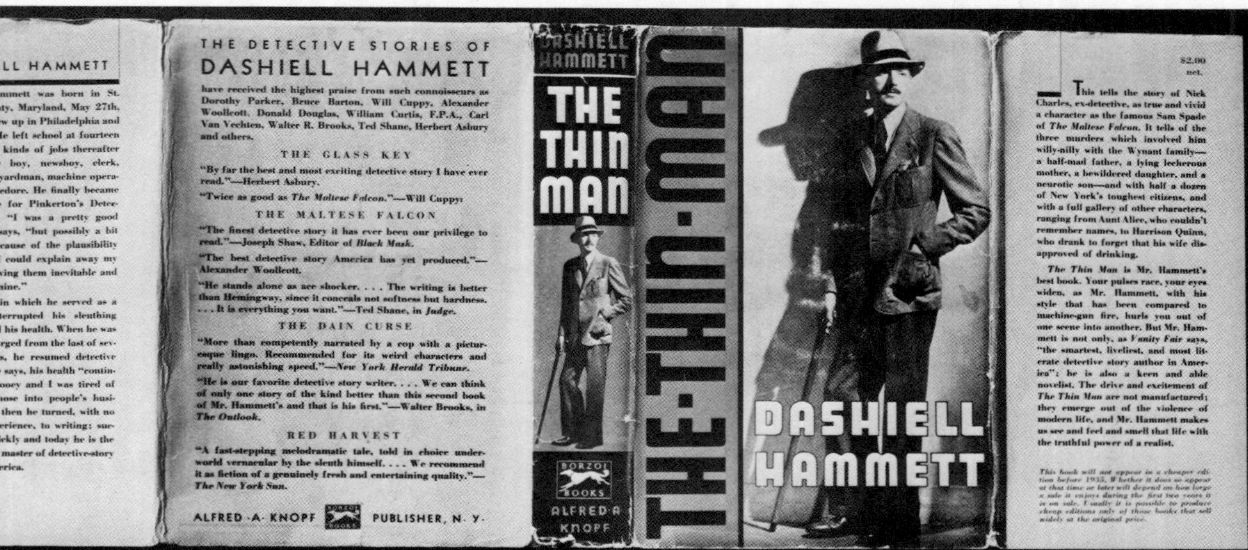

Dust jacket for A 6.1.a

A 6.1.g
Seventh printing (1935)

DASHIELL HAMMETT | [tapered rule] | THE | THIN MAN | [diamond device] | [tapered rule] | GROSSET & DUNLAP | Publishers NEW YORK

Copyright page: 'First and Second Printings Before Publication | Published January 8, 1934 | Third Printing January, 1934 | Fourth Printing January, 1934 | Fifth Printing January, 1934 | Sixth Printing March, 1934 | Seventh Printing July, 1934'.

March 1935.

Note: Copyright page of 1943 Pocket Books edition (A 6.6.a) notes 5 Grosset & Dunlap printings between March 1935 and April 1939.

A 6.1.h
Eighth printing (1940)

DASHIELL HAMMETT | [tapered rule] | THE | THIN | MAN | [diamond device] | [6-line notice that book was produced under wartime conditions, bordered on either side by decorative device] | [tapered rule] | GROSSET & DUNLAP | Publishers NEW YORK | By Arrangement with Alfred A. Knopf, Inc.

1940.

Note 1: Also noted without notice about wartime conditions.

Note 2: 1943 Pocket Books edition (A 6.6.a) notes 2 Grosset & Dunlap printings—one in December 1942, another in February 1943.

A 6.1.i
Ninth printing: The Complete Dashiell Hammett. New York: Knopf, 1942.

See AA 1.c.

A 6.1.j
Tenth printing (1946)

[within 4 ovals] A BLACK | WIDOW | [spider] | THRILLER | [outside ovals] [decorated rule] | The Thin Man | BY *Dashiell Hammett* | [decorated rule] | ALFRED • A • KNOPF | NEW YORK

Copyright page: 'First issued as a BLACK WIDOW THRILLER July 1946'.

A 6.2
Second edition (1934)

SIX | REDBOOK | NOVELS | [square with drawing of woman] | DASHIELL HAMMETT • MIGNON G. EBERHART • SIR PHILIP GIBBS • JAMES WARNER BELLAH • AGATHA CHRISTIE • CHARLES L. CLIFFORD

New York: McCall, 1934 (published February or March).

Note: Includes *The Thin Man* printed from *Redbook* magazine (December 1933) plates. Distributed to subscribers as a premium. Not for sale. *The Thin Man* was first published in *Redbook* magazine. *Six Redbook Novels,* published after the Knopf first book publication of the novel, was printed from the plates of the magazine publication. *Six Redbook Novels* is, therefore, the first book publication from the first setting of type of *The Thin Man.*

A 6.3
Third edition, first English printing (1934)

THE THIN MAN

By
DASHIELL HAMMETT

LONDON
ARTHUR BARKER LTD.
21 GARRICK STREET
COVENT GARDEN

A 6.3: 7³⁄₁₆″ × 4¹¹⁄₁₆″

First printed . . . 1934

PRINTED IN GREAT BRITAIN BY THE EDINBURGH PRESS, EDINBURGH

[A] B–I K–S⁸

[1–6] 7–284 [285–288]

Contents: p. 1: half title; p. 2: blank; p. 3: title; p. 4: copyright; p. 5: dedication; p. 6: disclaimer; pp. 7–284: text, headed '[rule] | THE THIN MAN | [rule] | I'; p. 285: blank; p. 286: colophon; pp. 287–288: blank.

Typography and paper: $5^1/_2$" ($5^3/_4$") × $3^1/_2$". 31 lines per page. Running heads: rectos and versos, 'THE THIN MAN'. Wove paper.

Binding: Orange V cloth (smooth) stamped in black. Front: 'THE | THIN MAN | [outline drawing of man] *Dashiell Hammett'.* Spine: 'THE | THIN MAN | Dashiell | Hammett | BARKER'. Back: blank. Wove endpapers. Top and front edges trimmed.

Dust jacket: Not seen.

Publication: 7s. 6d. Published May 1934.

Printing: Printed in Edinburgh by The Edinburgh Press.

Locations: BL ('14 MAY 34'); Bod ('MAY 18 1934'); RL.

A6.4
Fourth edition (1934)

THE THIN MAN | [tapered rule] | Dashiell Hammett | [tapered rule] | [Penguin seal] | PENGUIN BOOKS | *London*

Copyright page: '*First printed* . . . 1934 | *Published in Penguin Books* 1935'.

A6.5
Fifth edition: London: Heinemann, 1940.

Not seen.

A6.6.a
Sixth edition, first printing (1943)

[within shaded-rules frame, with 5 rules on left and bottom, 7 rules on top and right] THE | THIN MAN | [rule] | DASHIELL HAMMETT | ['pb' in reverse printing on black circle] | POCKET ['BOOKS' in hollow letters] BOOKS INC. | New York

Copyright page: '1st PRINTING [5 dots] DECEMBER, 1942'.

1943. #196.

Reprints noted: 18 printings, the last of which was November 1945. Title-page changes first noted in sixteenth printing: '[within shaded single-rule frame] THE THIN MAN | *by* | *DASHIELL HAMMETT* | [Pocket Books seal] | Pocket BOOKS, Inc. | New York, N.Y.'

A 6.7
Seventh edition (1947)

THE THIN MAN | *by* | DASHIELL HAMMETT | [device] | [Heinemann seal] | [short rule] | WILLIAM HEINEMANN LTD | LONDON :: TORONTO

Copyright page: 'FIRST PUBLISHED 1934 | REPRINTED FOUR TIMES | THIS EDITION 1947'.

A 6.8
Eighth edition: The Dashiell Hammett Omnibus. London, Toronto, Melbourne, Sydney, Wellington: Cassell, 1950.

See AA 3.

A 6.9
Ninth edition (1952)

THE THIN MAN | [tapered rule] | *Dashiell Hammett* | PENGUIN BOOKS | HARMONDSWORTH • MIDDLESEX

Copyright page: 'Reprinted 1952'.

A 6.10
Tenth edition: London: Heinemann, 1957.

Not seen.

A 6.11
Eleventh edition: Harmondsworth: Penguin, 1961.

Not seen.

A 6.12
Twelfth edition (1964)

[device] | THE | Maltese Falcon | & | The | Thin Man | BY | DASHIELL HAMMETT | [Vintage seal] | VINTAGE BOOKS | *A Division of Random House* | NEW YORK

Copyright page: 'FIRST VINTAGE EDITION, *March, 1964'.*

V-255.

A 6.13
Thirteenth edition: The Novels of Dashiell Hammett. New York: Knopf, 1965.

See AA 4.

A 6.14
Fourteenth edition (1966)

[all within single-rule frame] [2 lines in hollow letters within single-rule frame] DASHIELL | HAMMETT | [2 lines in reverse printing against black background] THE | THIN MAN | [within single-rule frame] A DELL BOOK

Copyright page: 'First Dell Printing—July, 1966'.

New York. # 8719.

A 6.15
Fifteenth edition (1972)

The | Thin Man | DASHIELL HAMMETT | [Vintage seal] | VINTAGE BOOKS | *A Division of Random House* | NEW YORK

Copyright page: 'Vintage Books Edition, May 1972'.

A 6.16
Sixteenth edition (1974)

THE THIN MAN | [rule] | *BY* | DASHIELL HAMMETT | [fingerprint] | A FINGERPRINT BOOK | [rule] | HAMISH HAMILTON | LONDON

1974.

A 6.17
Seventeenth edition (1974)

THE THIN MAN | [tapered rule] | DASHIELL HAMMETT | PENGUIN BOOKS

Copyright page: 'First published 1932 | Published in Penguin Books 1935 | Reprinted 1952, 1961, 1974 (twice)'.

Harmondsworth.

A 7 SECRET AGENT X-9 BOOK ONE

A 7.1
First edition (1934)

SECRET AGENT X-9

by

Dashiell Hammett

BOOK ONE

Illustrations by

Alex Raymond

Philadelphia

DAVID McKAY COMPANY

Washington Square

A 7.1: 7 3/8″ × 7 15/16″

Side stapled.

[1–2] 3–80

Contents: p. 1: title; p. 2: copyright; pp. 3–80: text.

Typography and paper: 6[15]/16" × 9[1]/16". 3 or 4 panels per page. Wove paper.

Binding: Printed boards. Front: '[1 line against orange background in hollow letters] SECRET AGENT X-9 | [thick black rule] | [panel from comic strip depicting a woman and 2 men, one of whom has just been shot by gun pointing through broken window] | [within single-rule frame] By DASHIELL HAMMETT'. Spine covered with unprinted red cloth. Back: same as front. All edges trimmed.

Publication: Unknown number of copies of the first printing. 25¢. Published 25 July 1934. Copyright 21 July 1934. Copyright #A151784.

Printing: Plates by Westcott & Thomson, Philadelphia; printing and binding by Kingsport Press, Kingsport, Tennessee.

Note: *Secret Agent X-9* first appeared as a syndicated comic strip in newspapers; see D 15–D 89.

Locations: LC ('JUL 21 1934', rebound); OP; SFACA.

Front cover for A 7.1

A 7.2
Second edition (1976)

[within triple-rules frame] [within double-rules circle] The detective classic | from the comics' Golden Age. | SECRET AGENT | X-9 | [drawing of men around card table in shoot-out with police] | [outside circle] By | Alex Raymond | & | Dashiell Hammett | [outside frame] Nostalgia Press, Inc., Box 293, Franklin Square, New York, 11010 | *Copyright 1976 Nostalgia Press, Inc., and King Features Syndicate*

Note: Includes all of *Book One,* all of *Book Two,* and adds material from the newspaper publication of the comic strip. See C 137, D 15–D 405.

A 8 SECRET AGENT X-9 BOOK TWO

A 8.1
First edition (1934)

SECRET AGENT X-9

by

Dashiell Hammett

BOOK TWO

Illustrations by

Alex Raymond

Philadelphia

DAVID McKAY COMPANY

Washington Square

A 8.1: 7 3/8" × 7 15/16"

Side stapled.

[1–2] 3–120

Contents: p. 1: title; p. 2: copyright; pp. 3–120: text.

Typography and paper: 6 15/16″ × 9 1/16″. 3 or 4 panels per page. Wove paper.

Binding: Printed boards. Front: '[1 line against yellow background in hollow letters] SECRET X-9 | [thick black rule] | [panel from comic strip depicting 3 people against background of flames and smoke] | [within single-rule frame] By DASHIELL HAMMETT [an orange circle on either side of frame] [within circle on left] 25 | CENTS [within circle on right] BOOK | 2'. Spine covered with unprinted blue cloth. Back: same as front except that price is omitted. All edges trimmed.

Publication: Unknown number of copies of the first printing. 25¢. Published in 1934. Copyright records not located.

Printing: Assumed to be as *Book One*.

Note: *Secret Agent X-9* first appeared as a syndicated comic strip in newspapers; see D 90–D 211.

Locations: OP; SFACA.

Front cover for A 8.1

A 8.2
Second edition (1976)

[within triple-rules frame] [within double-rules circle] The detective classic | from the comics' Golden Age. | SECRET AGENT | X-9 | [drawing of men around card table in shoot-out with police] | [outside circle] By | Alex Raymond | & | Dashiell Hammett | [outside frame] Nostalgia Press, Inc., Box 293, Franklin Square, New York, 11010 | *Copyright 1976 Nostalgia Press, Inc., and King Features Syndicate*

Note: Includes all of *Book One,* all of *Book Two,* and adds material from the newspaper publication of the comic strip. See C 137, D 15–D 405.

A 9 $106,000 BLOOD MONEY

A 9.1
First edition (1943)

$106,000
BLOOD MONEY
by
DASHIELL HAMMETT
LAWRENCE E. SPIVAK
Publisher

A 9.1: 7⁵⁄₈″ × 5⁵⁄₁₆″

Titles for the Bestseller Mystery are chosen from those mysteries which have had a large and continuing sale. Sometimes they are reprinted in full, but more often they are cut to speed up the story — always, of course, with the permission of the author or his publisher. This mystery has not been cut.

Bestseller Mystery, No. B40 . . . 570 Lexington Avenue, New York.
Manufactured in the United States of America.

Copyright, 1927, by Pro-Distributors Publishing Co., Inc. Reprinted by special arrangement with Dashiell Hammett.

[1–4]^{16}

[1–2] 3–126 [127–128]

Contents: p. 1: title; p. 2: copyright; pp. 3–126: text, headed 'CHAPTER ONE'; p. 127: advertisements; p. 128: blank.

Typography and paper: $5^{13}/_{16}$" (6") × $4^{1}/_{8}$". 29 or 30 lines per page. Running heads: rectos, '$106,000 BLOOD MONEY'; versos, 'DASHIELL HAMMETT'. Wove paper.

Binding: Deep reddish orange wrappers. Front: '[1 line against black background, printed in white] *Bestseller Mystery* | [following 6 lines against shaded white panel, printed in black and red] [black dollar sign against red money bags] [black] $106,000 | [red] BLOOD [black] MONEY | [red] BY | [black] *Dashiell Hammett* | [red] *Author of THE THIN MAN and THE MALTESE FALCON—* | *one of the greatest writers of mystery fiction of all time* • | [black drawing of mask and gun by '*Salter*'] | [thin white rule] | [black] 25¢'. Spine: '[vertically] [black] $106,000 BLOOD MONEY • *Dashiell Hammett* | [white] *Bestseller Mystery*'. Back: '[black book] [white] *BM* | [black gun] | [war-bond advertisement]'. All edges trimmed.

Publication: Unknown number of copies of the first printing. 25¢. Published 15 June 1943.

Note: Consists of "The Big Knockover" and "$106,000 Blood Money" collected as a novel; see C 67 and C 72.

Locations: OKentC; RL.

A 9.2.a
Second edition, first printing (1943)

Not seen.

A 9.2.b
Second edition, second printing (1944)

Blood Money | BY DASHIELL HAMMET | [Tower seal] CLEVELAND AND NEW YORK | THE WORLD PUBLISHING COMPANY

Copyright page: 'TOWER BOOKS EDITION | *First Printing October 1943* | *Second Printing January 1944* | HC'.

#T263.

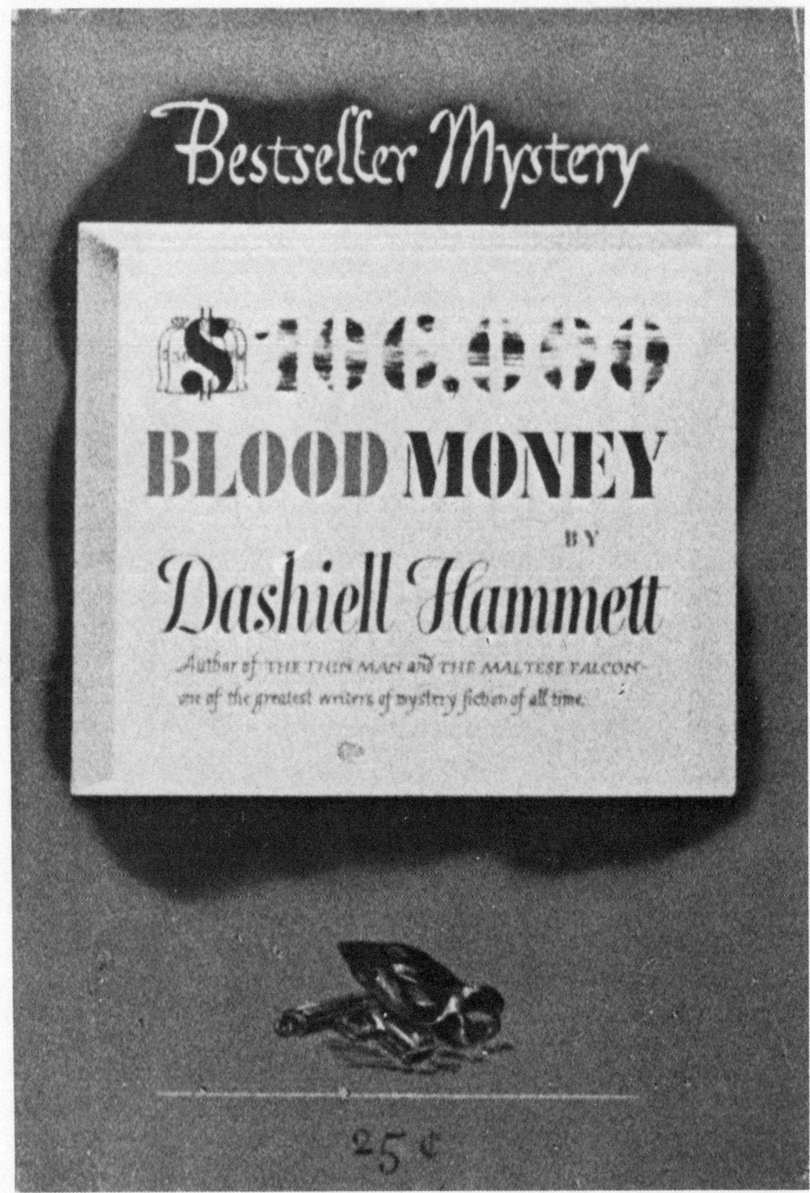

Front wrapper for A 9.1

A 9.3.a
Third edition, first printing (1944)

A *PRIVATE OPERATIVE* MURDER STORY | [dotted rule] | BLOOD | MONEY | By DASHIELL HAMMETT | Author of "The Maltese Falcon," | "The Thin Man," "Red Harvest," | "The Glass Key," etc. | [rule] | DELL PUBLISHING COMPANY | George T.

Delacorte, Jr., *President* • Helen Meyer, *Vice-President* | 149 Madison Avenue *Printed in U.S.A.* New York 16, N.Y.

1944. #53.

A 9.3.b
Third edition, second printing (1951)

A *CONTINENTAL OP* MURDER MYSTERY | [dotted rule] | BLOOD | MONEY | *By* DASHIELL HAMMETT | Author of | "Red Harvest" | "The Thin Man" | "The Glass Key" | "The Maltese Falcon" | [rule] | DELL PUBLISHING COMPANY, INC. | George T. Delacorte, Jr. Albert P. Delacorte Helen Meyer | *President Vice-President Vice-President* | 261 Fifth Avenue *Printed in U.S.A.* New York 16, N.Y. | DESIGNED AND PRODUCED BY WESTERN PRINTING & LITHOGRAPHING COMPANY

1951. #486.

A 9.4
Fourth edition (1948)

A DASHIELL HAMMETT *Detective* | [8 lines within octagonal double-rules frame] THE BIG KNOCK-OVER | *Originally published under the title* | $106,000 BLOOD MONEY | by DASHIELL HAMMETT | Author of: | *The Thin Man* | *The Maltese Falcon* | *Nightmare Town* | LAWRENCE E. SPIVAK, *Publisher*

1948. New York. Jonathan Press Mystery #J 36.

A 10 THE BATTLE OF THE ALEUTIANS
1944

THE BATTLE OF THE ALEUTIANS

In honor and memory of the men of the North Pacific Theater who died so that a continent might be free

★ ★ ★

A chain of unsinkable aircraft carriers now stretches across the North Pacific — from the shores of Alaska to the threshold of Japan. This small book is a partial record of the men who fought for these Aleutian bases, and the men who built them into impregnable fortresses that history will remember as the Northern Highway to Victory.

A 10: 5 7/16″ × 7 15/16″

* * * * *

PRODUCED BY THE INTELLIGENCE SECTION,
FIELD FORCE HEADQUARTERS, ADAK, ALASKA
OCTOBER, 1943

MAJOR HENRY W. HALL, Infantry
Intelligence Officer

Illustrations, maps and layout . SGT. HARRY FLETCHER

Written by . . . . CPL. DASHIELL HAMMETT
CPL. ROBERT COLODNY

Reproduction by detachment 29th Engineers stationed
with Headquarters Western Defense Command
1944

Stapled.

[1–24]

Contents: p. 1: title; p. 2: publication information; p. 3: epigraph; p. 4: map of Aleutian Islands; pp. 5–24: text.

Typography and paper: $3^7/_8$″ × 6″. 21 or 22 lines per page. No running heads. Wove paper.

Binding: Blue wrappers. Front: '[2 lines in white against black background] The Battle of | the Aleutians . . . | [black letters] A GRAPHIC HISTORY [star] 1942–1943'. Back: blank. All edges trimmed.

Publication: Unknown number of copies published in 1944.

Printing: 'Reproduction by detachment 29th Engineers stationed with Headquarters Western Defense Command 1944'.

Note: Text by Hammett, captions by Robert Colodny.

Location: RL.

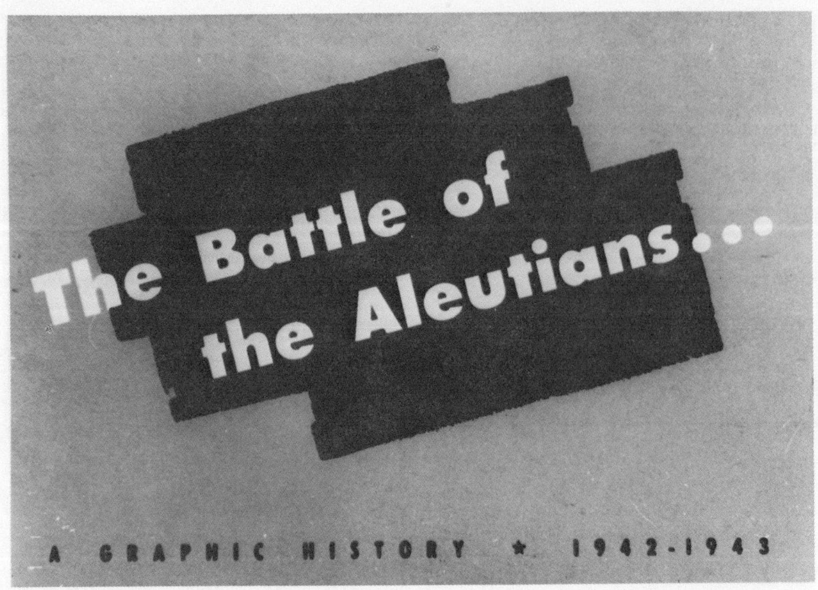

Front wrapper for A10

A 11 THE ADVENTURES OF SAM SPADE

A 11.1.a
First edition, first printing (1944)

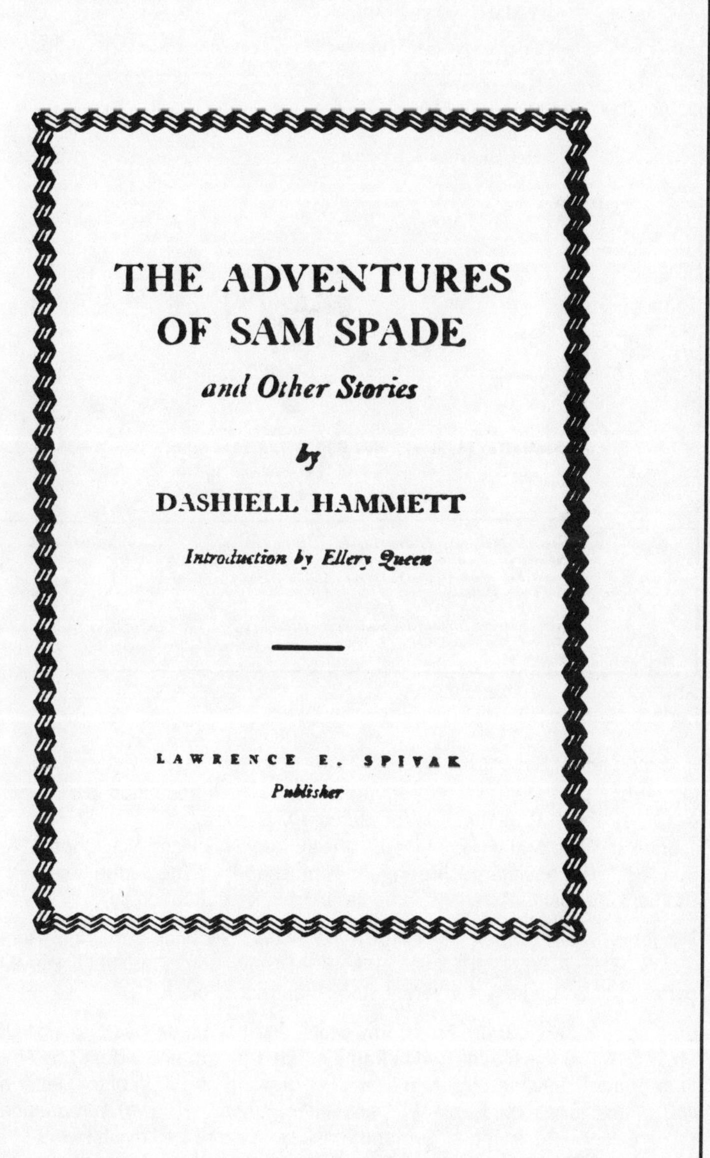
THE ADVENTURES OF SAM SPADE
and Other Stories
by
DASHIELL HAMMETT
Introduction by Ellery Queen
LAWRENCE E. SPIVAK
Publisher

A 11.1.a: 7 5/8″ × 5 5/16″

TABLE OF CONTENTS

Bestseller Mystery, No. B50 . . . 570 Lexington Avenue, New York 22.

Copyright, 1944, by The American Mercury, Inc.

Manufactured in the United States of America.

Copyright, 1924, 1926, by Pro-Distributor's Publishing Co., [illegible] Publishing Co.; copyright, 1932, 1934, by P. F. Collier and Son [illegible] League Publishers; copyright, 1943, by Dashiell Hammett. Reprinted by special arrangement with Dashiell Hammett.

Acknowledgment is gratefully made to the following magazines where these stories originally appeared: Black Mask; Collier's; The American Magazine; Mystery League. These stories have not been cut.

Perfect bound.

[1–2] 3–125 [126–128]

Contents: p. 1: title; p. 2: copyright; pp. 3–5: introduction by Ellery Queen; pp. 6–125: text; pp. 126–128: ads for Mercury Mysteries.

Stories: *"Too Many Have Lived," *"They Can Only Hang You Once," "A Man Called Spade," *"The Assistant Murderer," *"Nightshade," *"The Judge Laughed Last," *"His Brother's Keeper." (Asterisks indicate first book publication.)

Typography and paper: 5⁷/₈" (6¹/₁₆") × 4⁵/₁₆". 35 lines per page. Running heads: rectos, 'THE ADVENTURES OF SAM SPADE'; versos, 'DASHIELL HAMMETT'. Wove paper (first 96 pages on different stock than rest of book).

Binding: Brown paper. Front: '[in white against black background] *BESTSELLER MYSTERY* | [5 lines within white frame shaded on top and sides] *The Adventures* | *of Sam Spade* [drawing of gun in brown] | [drawing of gun in black, lettering in brown] *and other stories by* | [black] Dashiell Hammett | [brown] *Introduction by* [black] *Ellery Queen* | [drawing of gun and mask by 'Salter'] | [thin white rule] | 25¢'. Spine: '[vertically] *The Adventures of Sam Spade by Dashiell Hammett* [white] *Bestseller Mystery* | [horizontally, in black] B50'. Back: '[black drawing of book] [white lettering]

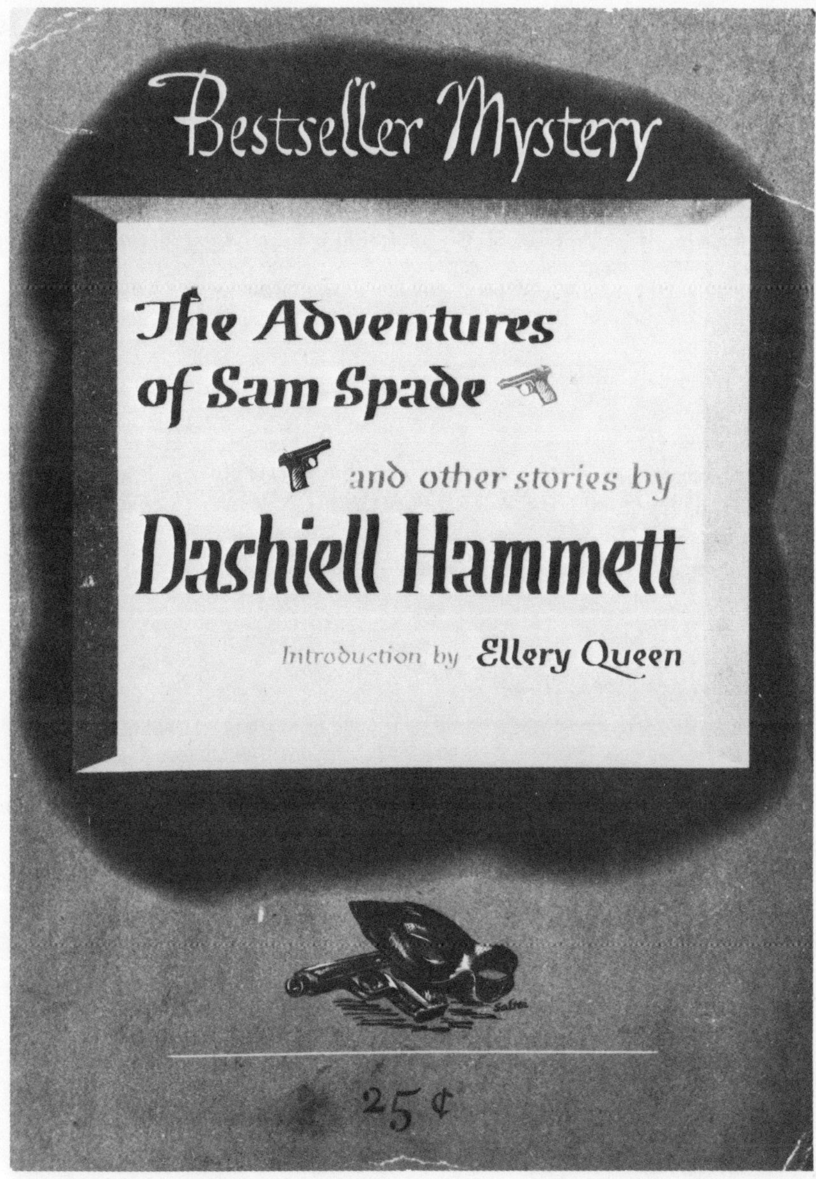

Front wrapper for A 11.1.a

BM | [drawing of gun] | [4 lines within white frame, white on black] PLEDGE YOURSELF TO BUY | [silhouette of white figure surrounded by stars] | [white rule] | U.S. WAR BONDS REGULARLY'.

Publication: Unknown number of copies of the first printing. 25¢. Published 14 April 1944.

Note: All stories in this volume first appeared in magazines; see C 123, C 124, C 122, C 61, C 126, C 30, and C 130.

Location: RL.

A 11.1.b
Second printing (1949)

THEY CAN ONLY | HANG YOU ONCE | *and Other Stories* | *Originally published under the title* THE ADVENTURES OF SAM SPADE | BY | DASHIELL HAMMETT | Author of: | *The Maltese Falcon* | *Nightmare Town* | *The Big Knockover* | [2 script 'M's within circle] | *A MERCURY MYSTERY* | THE AMERICAN MERCURY • NEW YORK | LAWRENCE E. SPIVAK, *Publisher*

1949.

A 11.2
Second edition (1945)

DASHIELL HAMMETT | *THE ADVENTURES OF* | *SAM SPADE* | *AND OTHER STORIES* | [Tower seal] | *THE WORLD PUBLISHING COMPANY* | *CLEVELAND AND NEW YORK*

Copyright page: 'TOWER BOOKS EDITION | *First Printing January* 1945 | HC'.

T-334.

A 11.3.a
Third edition, first printing (1945)

PRIVATE DETECTIVE MYSTERY STORIES | [dotted rule] | A MAN CALLED | SPADE | and Other Stories | By DASHIELL HAMMETT | Author of "The Maltese Falcon," | "The Thin Man," "Blood Money," | "The Continental OP," etc. | [rule] | DELL PUBLISHING COMPANY | George T. Delacorte, Jr., *President* Helen Meyer, *Vice-President* | 149 Madison Avenue *Printed in U.S.A.* New York 16, N.Y.

Contents: Adds "Meet Sam Spade," by Ellery Queen, and omits "Nightshade" and "The Judge Laughed Last."

1945. #90.

A 11.3.b
Third edition, second printing (1950)

PRIVATE DETECTIVE MYSTERY STORIES | [dotted rule] | A MAN CALLED | SPADE | and Other Stories | By DASHIELL HAMMETT | Author of "The Maltese Falcon," | "The Thin Man," "Blood Money," | "The Continental OP," etc. | [rule] | DELL PUBLISHING COMPANY, INC. | George T. Delacorte, Jr. Albert P. Delacorte Helen Meyer | *President Vice-President Vice-President* | 261 Fifth Avenue *Printed in U.S.A.* New York 16, N.Y. | DESIGNED AND PRODUCED BY WESTERN PRINTING & LITHOGRAPHING COMPANY

Dell #411 and later #452.

THEY CAN ONLY HANG YOU ONCE

(THE ADVENTURES OF SAM SPADE)

BY DASHIELL HAMMETT

INTRODUCTION BY ELLERY QUEEN

Front wrapper for A 11.1.b

A 12 THE CONTINENTAL OP

A 12.1
First edition (1945)

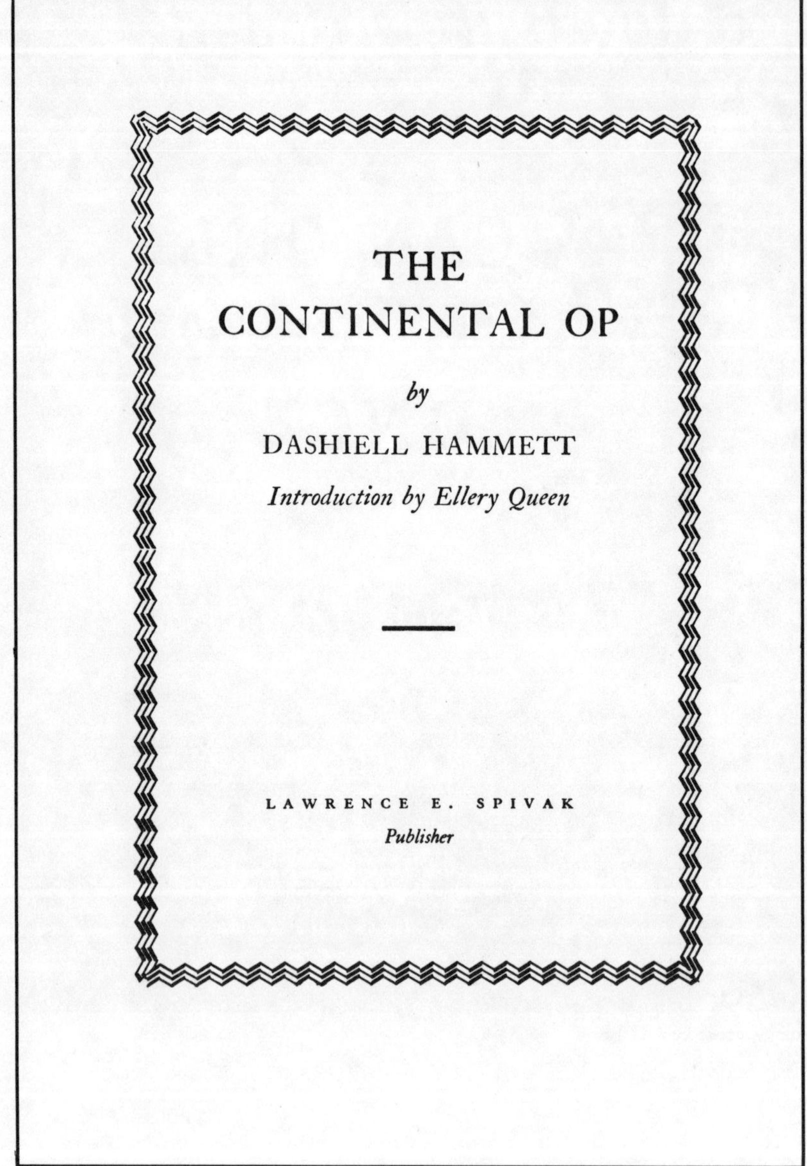

THE
CONTINENTAL OP

by

DASHIELL HAMMETT

Introduction by Ellery Queen

LAWRENCE E. SPIVAK
Publisher

A 12.1: $7\frac{5}{8}'' \times 5\frac{5}{16}''$

This book is manufactured in strict conformity with Government regulations for saving paper.

TABLE OF CONTENTS

Bestseller Mystery, No. B62 . . . 570 Lexington Avenue, New York 22.
Copyright, 1945, by The American Mercury, Inc.
Manufactured in the United States of America.

Copyright, 1924, 1929, 1930 by Pro-Distributor's Publishing Co., Inc.
Reprinted by special arrangement with Dashiell Hammett.
Acknowledgment is gratefully made to BLACK MASK *magazine where these stories originally appeared. These stories have not been cut.*

Perfect binding.

[1–2] 3 [4–6] 7–126 [127–128]

Contents: p. 1: title; p. 2: contents and copyright; pp. 3–5: introduction by Ellery Queen; p. 6: blank; pp. 7–126: text; p. 127: advertisement; p. 128: blank.

Stories: "Fly Paper," *"Death on Pine Street," *"Zigzags of Treachery," "The Farewell Murder." (Asterisks indicate first book publication.)

Typography and paper: $5^3/_8$" ($5^9/_{16}$") × $4^1/_2$". 35 to 38 lines per page. Running heads: rectos, 'THE CONTINENTAL OP'; versos, 'DASHIELL HAMMETT'.

Binding: Medium greenish blue wrappers. Front: '[in white against black background] *Bestseller Mystery* | [8 lines against white panel edged in gray on three sides] [black] *The* | [white edged in black] CONTINENTAL [against blue badge] OP | *by* | DASHIELL HAMMETT | [blue] *Introduction by* ELLERY QUEEN | [black] *"Dashiell Hammett gave us the first truly* | *American detective story; he is our most important* | *modern originator."—Ellery Queen* | [black drawing of mask and gun by 'Salter'] |

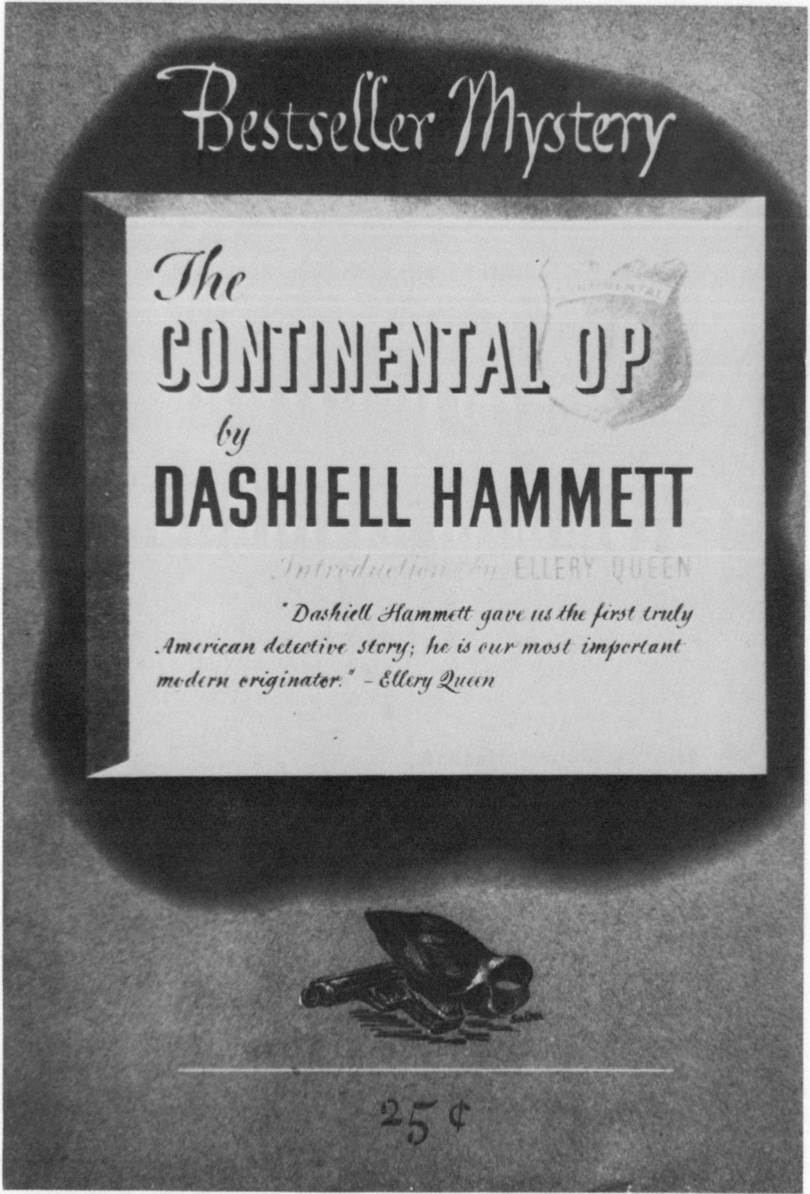

Front wrapper for A 12.1

[thin white rule] | [black] 25¢'. Spine: '[vertically] [black] *The Continental* OP *by Dashiell Hammett* [white] *Bestseller Mystery* [black] B62'. Back: Bestseller seal and war-bond ad. All edges trimmed.

Publication: Unknown number of copies of the first printing. 25¢. Published 13 April 1945. Copyright 13 April 1945. Copyright #AA 489983.

Printing: Plates, printing, and binding by The Rumford Press.

Note: All stories in this volume first appeared in magazines; see C 106, C 42, C 33, and C 114.

Locations: DLC ('MAY 23 1949'); InU; OKentC; RL.

A 12.2
Second edition (1946)

PRIVATE DETECTIVE MURDER STORIES | [dotted rule] | THE | CONTINENTAL | OP | *By* DASHIELL HAMMETT | Author of "A Man Called Spade," | "The Maltese Falcon," "The Glass Key," | "The Thin Man," "The Return of the | Continental Op," etc. | [rule] | DELL PUBLISHING COMPANY | George T. Delacorte, Jr., *President* • Helen Meyer, *Vice-President* | 149 Madison Avenue *Printed in U.S.A.* New York 16, N.Y.

1946. #129.

A 12.3
Third edition (1949)

A DASHIELL HAMMETT *Detective* | [6 lines within double-ruled octagon] THE CONTINENTAL OP | by DASHIELL HAMMETT | Author of: | *Nightmare Town* | *They Can Only Hang You Once* | INTRODUCTION BY ELLERY QUEEN | LAWRENCE E. SPIVAK, *Publisher*

4 January 1949. New York. #J40.

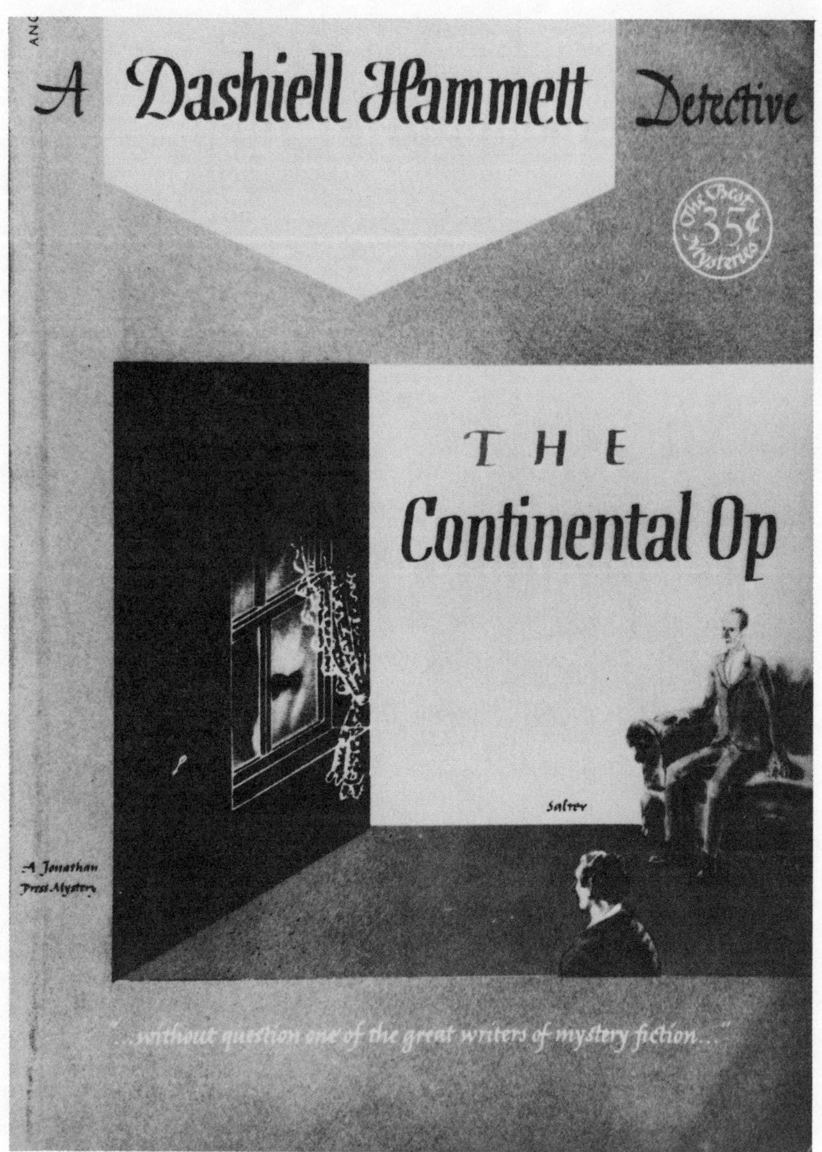

Front wrapper for A 12.3

A 13 THE RETURN OF THE CONTINENTAL OP

A 13.1
First edition (1945)

A DASHIELL HAMMETT *Detective*

THE RETURN OF THE CONTINENTAL OP

by DASHIELL HAMMETT

LAWRENCE E. SPIVAK, *Publisher*

A 13.1: 7 5/8" × 5 5/16"

TABLE OF CONTENTS

A JONATHAN PRESS MYSTERY NO. J17 . . . *Published by The Jonathan Press, Inc., 570 Lexington Avenue, New York. Printed in the United States of America. These mysteries are sometimes reprinted in full, but more often they are cut to speed up the story — always, of course, with the permission of the author or his publisher. These stories have not been cut.*

Copyright, 1945 by The Jonathan Press Inc.; 1924, 1925, 1930 by Pro-Distributor's Publishing Co., Inc. Reprinted by special permission of Dashiell Hammett.

Acknowledgment is gratefully made to Black Mask magazine where these stories originally appeared

Perfect binding.

[1–2] 3–5 [6] 7–127 [128]

Contents: p. 1: title; p. 2: contents and copyright; pp. 3–5: introduction by Ellery Queen; p. 6: blank; pp. 7–127: text; p. 128: ad for Mercury, Jonathan, and Bestseller Mysteries.

Stories: *"The Whosis Kid," *"The Gutting of Couffignal," "Death and Company," *"One Hour," *"The Tenth Clue." (Asterisks indicate first book publication.)

Typography and paper: 5 13/16" (6 1/16") × 4 1/2". 35 lines per page. Running heads: rectos, 'THE RETURN OF THE CONTINENTAL OP'; versos, 'DASHIELL HAMMETT'. Wove paper.

Binding: Very red wrappers. Front: '*A* [2 words within brilliant yellow pentagon] *Dashiell Hammett Detective* | [white] A JONATHAN PRESS MYSTERY | [5 lines against white panel within 'Salter' drawing of shoe, typewriter, bullets, wallets, lock-box, and crossed-out question marks] [black] *The Return* | *of the* | *Continental* | *Op* | [red] *Introduction by Ellery Queen* | [black] *A Jonathan* | *Mystery* | 25¢ | [white] *Dashiell Hammett is without question one of the great writers of* | *mystery fiction and the leader in our generation.*' Spine: '[vertically] *A* [white] *Dashiell Hammett* [black] *Detective* [white] *The Return of the Continental Op* [black] *A Jonathan Mystery J 17*'. Back: black and white drawing of winged gun within circle. All edges trimmed.

Publication: Unknown number of copies of the first printing. 25¢. Published 6 July 1945. Copyright 6 July 1945. Copyright #AA 495785.

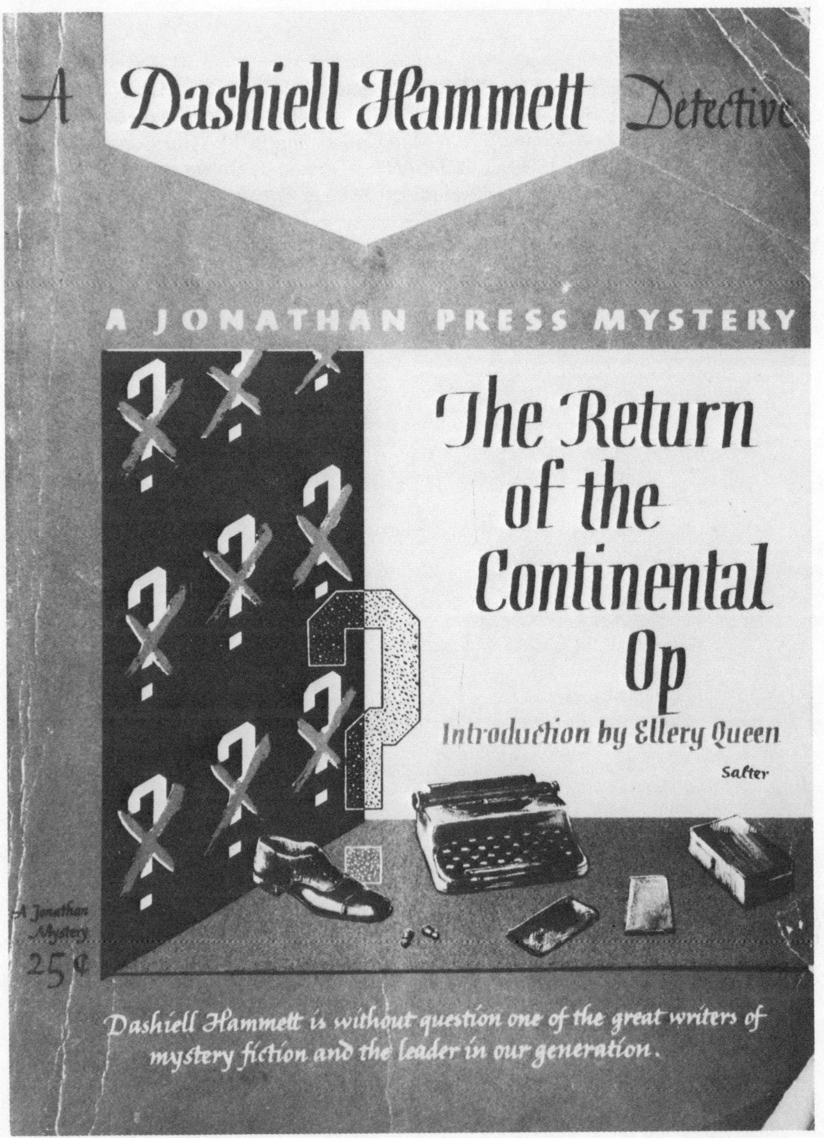

Front wrapper for A 13.1

Printing: Printing and binding by The Rumford Press.

Note: All stories in this volume first appeared in magazines; see C 49, C 59, C 120, C 36, and C 26.

Locations: InU; OKentC; RL.

A 13.2
Second edition (1947)

PRIVATE DETECTIVE MYSTERY STORIES | [dotted rule] | THE RETURN | OF THE | CONTINENTAL OP | *By* DASHIELL HAMMETT | Author of "The Maltese Falcon," | "The Thin Man," "Blood Money," | "A Man Called Spade," | "The Continental OP," etc. | [rule] | DELL PUBLISHING COMPANY | George T. Delacorte, Jr., *President* • Helen Meyer, *Vice-President* | 149 Madison Avenue *Printed in U.S.A.* New York 16, N.Y.

1947. #154.

A 14 HAMMETT HOMICIDES

A 14.1
First edition (1946)

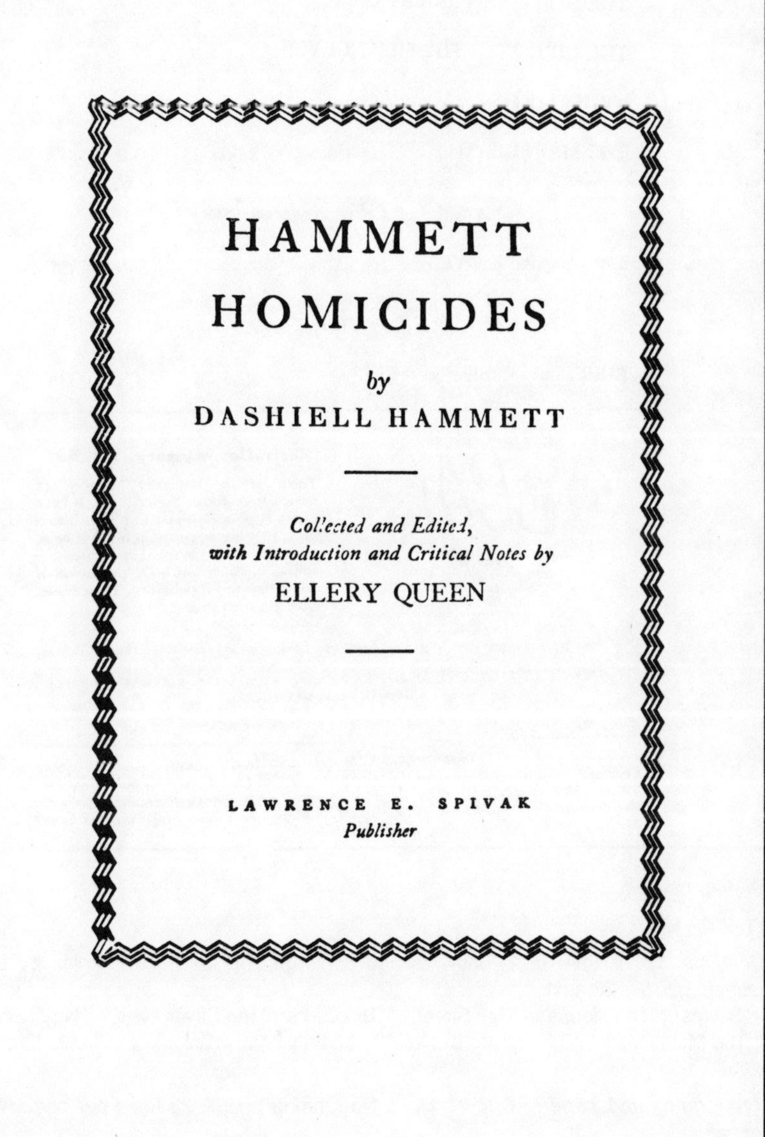
HAMMETT
HOMICIDES
by
DASHIELL HAMMETT
Collected and Edited,
with Introduction and Critical Notes by
ELLERY QUEEN
LAWRENCE E. SPIVAK
Publisher

A 14.1: $7^{5}/_{8}'' \times 5^{5}/_{16}''$

TABLE OF CONTENTS

Bestseller Mystery, No. B81

Titles for the Bestseller Mystery are chosen from those mysteries which have had a large and continuing sale. Sometimes they are reprinted in full, but more often they are cut to speed up the story — always, of course, with the permission of the author or his publisher. These stories have not been cut.

Published by the American Mercury, Inc., 570 Lexington Avenue, New York City 22.

The AMERICAN MERCURY Mystery Books: MERCURY MYSTERY, BESTSELLER MYSTERY, JONATHAN PRESS MYSTERY

COVER AND TYPOGRAPHY BY GEORGE SALTER

Copyright, 1946, by The American Mercury, Inc.
Copyright, 1924, 1927, by Pro-Distributor's Publishing Co., Inc.; 1925, by Sunset Magazine; and 1924 by Crowell Publishing Co. Reprinted by special arrangement with Dashiell Hammett.
Acknowledgment is gratefully made to Black Mask Magazine, Colliers Magazine, and Sunset Magazine, where these stories originally appeared.

Perfect binding.

[1–2] 3–128

Contents: p. 1: title; p. 2: contents and copyright; pp. 3–5: introduction by Ellery Queen; pp. 6–128: text.

Stories: *"The House in Turk Street," *"The Girl with the Silver Eyes," *"Night Shots," *"The Main Death," "Two Sharp Knives," "Ruffian's Wife." (Asterisks indicate first book publication.)

Typography and paper: $6^3/_8$" × $4^3/_{16}$". No running heads. 38 lines per page. Wove paper.

Binding: Medium yellow green wrappers. Front: '[American Mercury seal in white] | [against black background] *Bestseller Mystery* | [5 lines against white panel edged on 3 sides with gray, along with green drawings of weapons] [black] *Hammett* |

Front wrapper for A 14.1

Homicides | by Dashiell Hammett | "Who doesn't read him misses much of | modern America." DOROTHY PARKER | [black mask and gun] | [thin white rule] | [black] 25¢'. Spine: '[vertically] *Hammett Homicides* × *Dashiell Hammett* [white] *Bestseller Mystery* [black] B81'. Back: Bestseller Mystery seal. All edges trimmed.

Publication: Unknown number of copies of the first printing. 25¢. Published 20 December 1946. Copyright unknown. Copyright #AA 31995.

Note: All stories in this volume first appeared in magazines; see C 37, C 38, C 29, C 75, C 129, and C 56.

Locations: DLC ('DEC 27 1946'); OKentC; RL.

A 14.2
Second edition (1948)

DETECTIVE AND MURDER STORIES | [dotted rule] | HAMMETT | HOMICIDES | *By* DASHIELL HAMMETT | Author of "The Maltese Falcon," | "Red Harvest," "The Dain Curse," etc. | *Collected and Edited by* | ELLERY QUEEN | [rule] | DELL PUBLISHING COMPANY | George T. Delacorte, Jr., *President* • Helen Meyer, *Vice-President* | 149 Madison Avenue *Printed in U.S.A.* New York 16, N.Y. | DESIGNED AND PRODUCED BY WESTERN PRINTING & LITHOGRAPHING COMPANY

1948. #223.

A 15 DEAD YELLOW WOMEN

A 15.1
First edition (1947)

Ellery Queen Selects:

DEAD YELLOW WOMEN

by DASHIELL HAMMETT

Selected and Edited with
Introduction and Critical Notes by
ELLERY QUEEN

LAWRENCE E. SPIVAK, *Publisher*

A 15.1: $7^{5}/_{8}'' \times 5^{5}/_{16}''$

CONTENTS

A JONATHAN PRESS MYSTERY NO. J29 . . . *Published by the Jonathan Press, Inc., 570 Lexington Avenue, New York. Printed in the United States of America. This book was selected for us by Ellery Queen, famous for his bestselling books, movies and radio shows. Mr. Queen is also editor of Ellery Queen's Mystery Magazine. These mysteries are sometimes reprinted in full, but more often they are cut to speed up the story — always, of course, with the permission of the author or his publisher. These stories have not been cu...*

The AMERICAN MERCURY Mystery Books: MERCURY MYSTERY, BESTSELLER MYSTERY, JONATHAN PRESS MYSTERY.

COVER AND TYPOGRAPHY BY GEORGE SALTER

Perfect binding.

[1–2] 3–127 [128]

Contents: p. 1: title; p. 2: contents and copyright; pp. 3–5: introduction by Ellery Queen; pp. 6–127: text; p. 128: ads for Mercury Mysteries.

Stories: *"Dead Yellow Women," *"The Golden Horseshoe," *"House Dick," *"Who Killed Bob Teal?" "The Green Elephant," *"The Hairy One." (Asterisks indicate first book publication.)

Typography and paper: $6^{3}/_{16}$" ($6^{7}/_{16}$") × $4^{1}/_{2}$". 37 lines per page. Running heads: rectos, story titles; versos, 'DASHIELL HAMMETT'.

Binding: Green wrappers. Front: '[vertically] ANC | [yellow rectangle] [yellow script] Ellery Queen SELECTS: | [black against yellow pentagon] Dashiell Hammett's | [American Mercury seal in yellow against green background] | [drawing of room with dead woman and dying man in red, gray, black, and white by 'Salter'] [black against

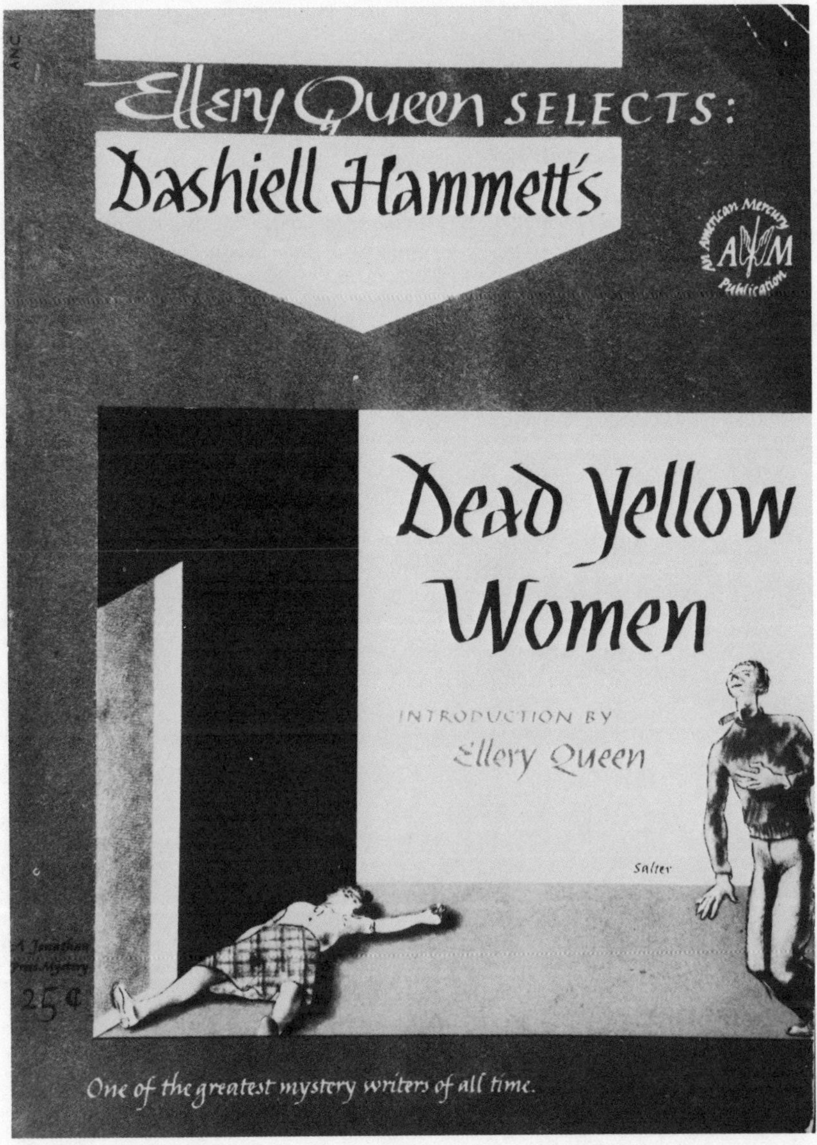

Front wrapper for A 15.1

white wall of room] Dead Yellow | Women | [in blue] *INTRODUCTION BY* | *Ellery Queen* | [black against green] *A Jonathan* | *Press Mystery* | 25¢ | [yellow] *One of the greatest mystery writers of all time.*' Spine: '[vertically] [black] *ELLERY QUEEN Selects:* [yellow] *Dead Yellow Women BY Dashiell Hammett* [black] *A Jonathan Press Mystery*'. Back: black gun with yellow wings within yellow circle.

Publication: Unknown number of copies of the first printing. 25¢. Published 22 July 1947.

Note: All stories in this volume were previously published in magazines; see C 58, C 45, C 24, C 44, C 20, and C 50.

Locations: DLC ('JUL 28 1947'); RL.

A 15.2.a
Second edition, first printing (1949)

DETECTIVE AND MURDER STORIES | [dotted rule] | DEAD | YELLOW | WOMEN | *By* DASHIELL HAMMETT | Author of "Hammett Homicides," | "The Continental Op," "Return | of the Continental Op," | "Adventures of Sam Spade," etc. | *Selected and Edited by* | ELLERY QUEEN | [rule] | DELL PUBLISHING COMPANY, INC. | George T. Delacorte, Jr. Albert P. Delacorte Helen Meyer | *President Vice-President Vice-President* | 261 Fifth Avenue *Printed in U.S.A.* New York 16, N.Y. | DESIGNED AND PRODUCED BY WESTERN PRINTING & LITHOGRAPHING COMPANY

1949. #308.

A 15.2.b
Second edition, second printing: New York: Dell, 1950.

#421.

A 16 NIGHTMARE TOWN

A 16.1
First edition (1948)

NIGHTMARE TOWN

BY

DASHIELL HAMMETT

COLLECTED AND EDITED, WITH AN INTRODUCTION BY

ELLERY QUEEN

A MERCURY MYSTERY

THE AMERICAN MERCURY • NEW YORK

LAWRENCE E. SPIVAK, *Publisher*

A 16.1: 7⁵/₈" × 5⁵/₁₆"

CONTENTS

***MERCURY MYSTERIES** are chosen from the hundreds of mysteries published every year — for their pace, literary quality and readability. Sometimes they are reprinted in full, but more often they are cut to increase the speed of the story — always, of course, with the permission of the author or his publisher. This book has not been cut.*

A MERCURY BOOK, NO. 120

Published by The AMERICAN MERCURY, Inc., 570 Lexington Ave., New York 22

The AMERICAN MERCURY Mystery Books: MERCURY MYSTERY, BESTSELLER MYSTERY, JONATHAN PRESS MYSTERY

Printed in the United States of America. Single copy 25¢. Twelve books $3.00

Copyright, 1948, by The American Mercury
CORKSCREW, *copyright, 1925, by Pro-Distributors, Co., Inc.;* THE SCORCHED FACE, *copyright, 1925, by Pro-Distributors, Co., Inc.;* ALBERT PASTOR AT HOME, *from Esquire, Autumn, 1933, copyright, 1933, by Esquire Inc., Esquire Building, Chicago, Ill.;* NIGHTMARE TOWN, *copyright, 1924, by the Frank A. Munsey Co. All stories reprinted by special permission of Dashiell Hammett.*

COVER AND TYPOGRAPHY BY GEORGE SALTER

Perfect binding.

[1–2] 3–128

Contents: p. 1: title; p. 2: contents and copyright; pp. 3–5: introduction by Ellery Queen; pp. 6–128: text.

Stories: *"Nightmare Town," *"The Scorched Face," *"Albert Pastor at Home," *"Corkscrew." (Asterisks indicate first book publication.)

Typography and paper: 6 3/8" (6 5/8") × 4 7/16". 37 lines per page. Running heads: rectos and versos, story titles.

Binding: Medium reddish brown wrappers. Front: '[white] [American Mercury seal] | *A* | *Mercury Mystery* [dagger] | [4 lines in black against background of 'Salter' drawing of bearded man on stamp] *Nightmare Town* | *by* | *Dashiell Hammett* | *INTRODUCTION BY Ellery Queen* | [white] *"Hammett achieves tremendous impact and virility."* | *HOWARD HAYCRAFT in "Murder for Pleasure"* | [thick short rule] | 25¢'. Spine: '[vertically] *A Mercury Mystery* • *Nightmare Town* × *Dashiell Hammett 120*'. Back: 'NIGHTMARE TOWN | [8-line comment on book] | [swash within drawn oval] M [dagger] M'.

Publication: Unknown number of copies of the first printing. 25¢. Published 10 February 1948. Copyright #AA 36835.

Note: All stories in this volume were previously published in magazines; see C 47, C 52, C 127, and C 55.

Locations: DLC ('FEB 17 1948'); InU; OKentC; RL.

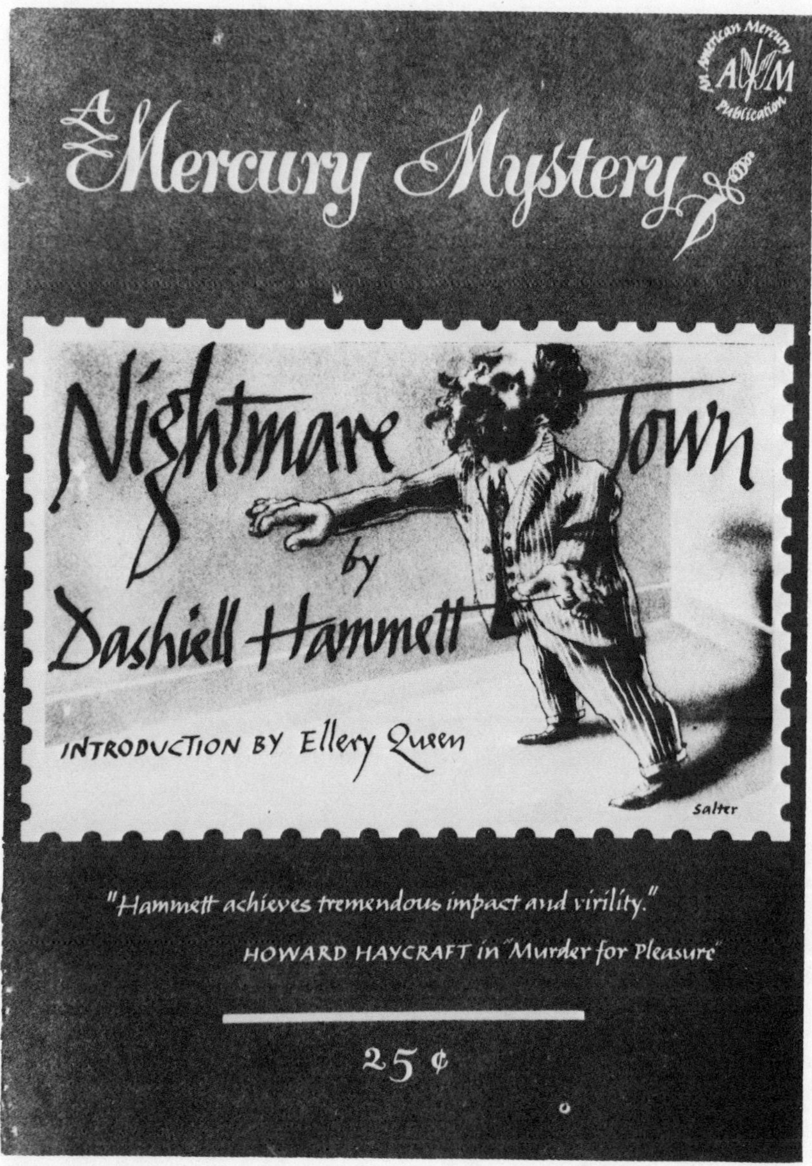

Front wrapper for A 16.1

A 16.2
Second edition (1950)

DETECTIVE AND MURDER STORIES | [dotted rule] | NIGHTMARE TOWN | *By* DASHIELL HAMMETT | Author of | "Dead Yellow Women," | "Hammett Homicides," | "The Continental Op," | "Return of the Continental Op," etc. | *Selected and Edited by* | ELLERY QUEEN | [rule] | DELL PUBLISHING COMPANY, INC. | George T. Delacorte,

Jr. Albert P. Delacorte Helen Meyer | *President Vice-President Vice-President* | 261 Fifth Avenue *Printed in U.S.A.* New York 16, N.Y. | DESIGNED AND PRODUCED BY WESTERN PRINTING & LITHOGRAPHING COMPANY

1950. #379.

A 17 THE CREEPING SIAMESE

A 17.1
First edition (1950)

A DASHIELL HAMMETT *Detective*

THE CREEPING SIAMESE

by DASHIELL HAMMETT

Collected and Edited, with Introduction by

ELLERY QUEEN

LAWRENCE E. SPIVAK, *Publisher*

A 17.1: 7⅝″ × 5$^{5}/_{16}$″

TABLE OF CONTENTS

A JONATHAN PRESS MYSTERY NO. J48 . . . *Published by The [illegible] Press, Inc., 570 Lexington Avenue, New York. Printed in the United [illegible] These mysteries are sometimes reprinted in full, but more often [illegible] to speed up the story — always, of course, with the permission of the author [illegible]. These stories have not been cut.*

The AMERICAN MERCURY Mystery Books: MERCURY MYSTERY, BESTSELLER MYSTERY, JONATHAN PRESS MYSTERY

COVER AND TYPOGRAPHY BY GEORGE SALTER
JOSEPH W. FERMAN, *General Manager*

Copyright, 1950, by The Jonathan Press, Inc.

THE CREEPING SIAMESE: *copyright, 1926, by Popular Publications, Inc.;* THE MAN WHO KILLED DAN ODAMS: *copyright, 1923, by Popular Publications, Inc.;* [illegible] NAILS IN MR. CAYTERER: *copyright, 1925, by Popular Publications, Inc.;* THE JOKE ON [illegible]: *copyright, 1949, by Tops Magazine, Inc.;* TOM, DICK OR HARRY: *[illegible] The World Publishing Company;* THIS KING BUSINESS: *copyright, 1927, by The Priscilla Company.*

Reprinted by special arrangement with Dashiell Hammett

PRINTED IN THE UNITED STATES OF AMERICA

[1–4][16]

[1–2] 3–127 [128]

Contents: p. 1: title; p. 2: contents and copyright; pp. 3–5: introduction by Ellery Queen; pp. 6–127: text; p. 128: ad page.

Stories: *"The Creeping Siamese," *"The Man Who Killed Dan Odams," *"The Nails in Mr. Cayterer," *"The Joke on Eloise Morey," "Tom, Dick or Harry," *"This King Business." (Asterisks indicate first book publication.)

Typography and paper: 4 7/16" × 6 11/16". 36 lines per page. No running heads. Wove paper.

Binding: Red wrappers. Front: 'A [2 words in yellow pentagon] Dashiell Hammett Detective | [white within white circle] The Best Mysteries 35¢ | [5 lines against white panel in drawing by Salter of man falling through door in green, blue, black, white, and brown] THE | Creeping Siamese | with an introduction by | ELLERY QUEEN | [against blue panel] COMPLETE AND UNABRIDGED | [to left of drawing] A Jonathan

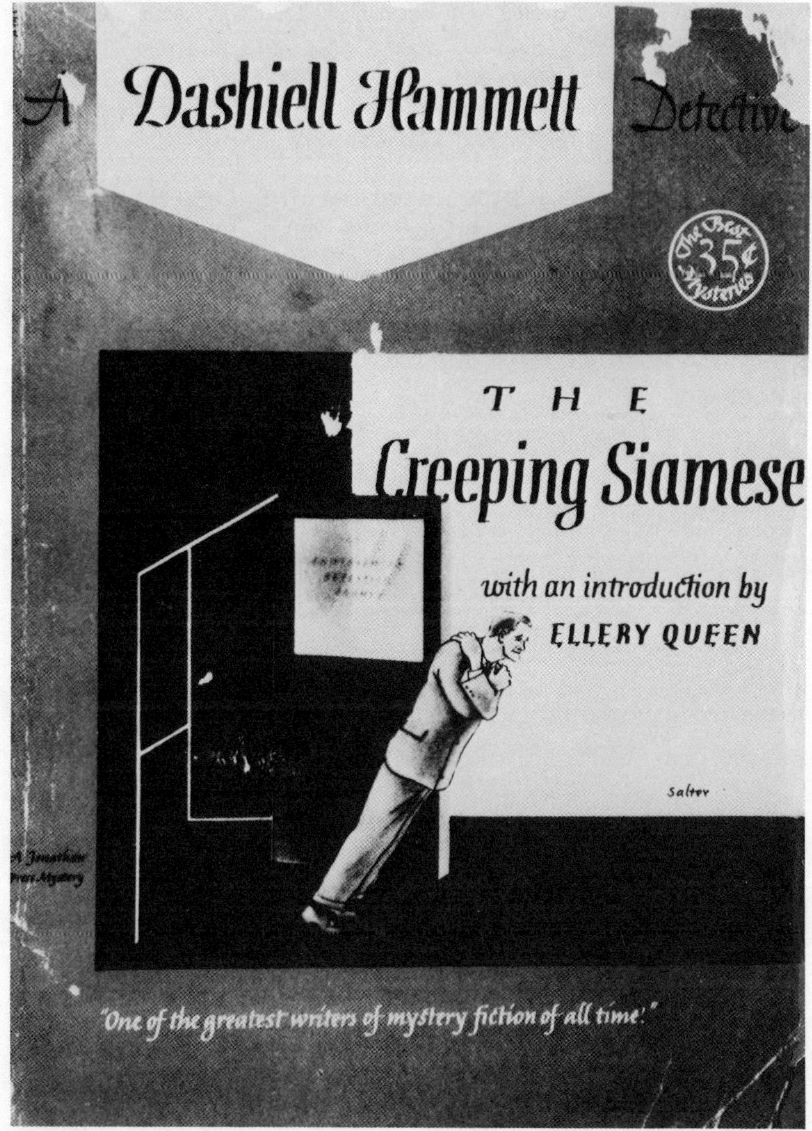

Front wrapper for A 17.1

Press Mystery | [beneath drawing] "One of the greatest writers of mystery fiction of all time." ' Spine: '[vertically] [black] A [white] Dashiell Hammett [black] Detective [white] The Creeping Siamese [black] A Jonathan Press Mystery [white] J48'. Back: '[white] THE CREEPING SIAMESE | [10-line blurb] | [black guns with white wings within white circle]'.

Publication: Unknown number of copies of the first printing. 35¢. Published 28 August 1950. Copyright #A47863.

Printing: Printing and binding by The Rumford Press.

Note: All stories in this volume were first published in magazines; see C 62, C 28, C 60, C 11, C 48, and C 82.

Locations: DLC ('SEP 13 1950'); RL.

A 17.2
Second edition (1951)

DETECTIVE AND MURDER STORIES | [dotted rule] | THE | CREEPING | SIAMESE | *By* DASHIELL HAMMETT | Author of "Nightmare Town," | "Dead Yellow Women," | "Hammett Homicides," etc. | *Selected and Edited by* | ELLERY QUEEN | COVER PAINTING BY ROBERT STANLEY | [rule] | DELL PUBLISHING COMPANY, INC. | George T. Delacorte, Jr. Albert P. Delacorte Helen Meyer | *President Vice-President Vice-President* | 261 Fifth Avenue *Printed in U.S.A.* New York 16, N.Y. | DESIGNED AND PRODUCED BY WESTERN PRINTING & LITHOGRAPHING COMPANY

1951. #538.

A 18 WOMAN IN THE DARK
Only edition (1951)

More Adventures of THE CONTINENTAL OP

WOMAN IN THE DARK

by DASHIELL HAMMETT

Collected and Edited,
with Introduction by
ELLERY QUEEN

COMPLETE AND UNABRIDGED

LAWRENCE E. SPIVAK, *Publisher*

A 18: 7 5/8″ × 5 5/16″

TABLE OF CONTENTS

JONATHAN PRESS MYSTERIES *are chosen from the hundreds of mysteries published every year — for their pace, literary quality and readability. Sometimes they are cut to speed up the story, with the permission of the author or his publisher, but more often they are reprinted in full — complete and unabridged. These stories have not been cut.*

A JONATHAN PRESS MYSTERY, NO. 59

Jonathan Press Mysteries, Mercury Mysteries, Bestseller Mysteries are published under the MERCURY IMPRINT

THE JONATHAN PRESS, INC., 570 Lexington Avenue, New York 22, N. Y.

Copyright, 1951, by The Jonathan Press, Inc.

ARSON PLUS: *copyright, 1923, by Dashiell Hammett;* SLIPPERY FINGERS: *copyright, 1923, by Dashiell Hammett;* THE BLACK HAT THAT WASN'T THERE: *copyright, 1923, by Dashiell Hammett;* WOMAN IN THE DARK: *copyright, 1934, by Dashiell Hammett;* AFRAID OF A GUN: *copyright, 1924, by Pro-Distributor's Publishing Co., Inc.;* HOLIDAY: *copyright, 1923, by Dashiell Hammett;* THE MAN WHO STOOD IN THE WAY: *copyright, 1923, by Dashiell Hammett.*

Reprinted by special arrangement with Dashiell Hammett

$[1\text{–}4]^{16}$

[1–2] 3–128

Contents: p. 1: title; p. 2: contents and copyright; pp. 3–9: introduction by Ellery Queen; pp. 10–128: text.

Stories: *"Arson Plus," *"Slippery Fingers," *"The Black Hat That Wasn't There," *"Woman in the Dark," *"Afraid of a Gun," *"Holiday," *"The Man Who Stood in the Way." (Asterisks indicate first book publication.)

Typography and paper: 6 9/16" (6 3/4") × 4 1/8". 36 lines per page. Running heads: rectos, 'WOMAN IN THE DARK'; versos, 'DASHIELL HAMMETT'. Wove paper.

Binding: Dark bluish green wrappers. Front: '[2 lines in black on brilliant yellow pentagon] *MORE ADVENTURES OF THE* | *Continental Op* | [white Mercury Publications seal] | [white] *FIRST BOOK COLLECTION OF THESE STORIES* | [5 lines within white panel against black, white, and green drawing of 3 people and ladder by 'Salter'] [black] *Woman* | *in the Dark* | [blue] *by Dashiell Hammett* | [black] *Introduction by Ellery Queen* | *A Jonathan* | *Press Mystery* | 35¢ | [1 line against green panel]

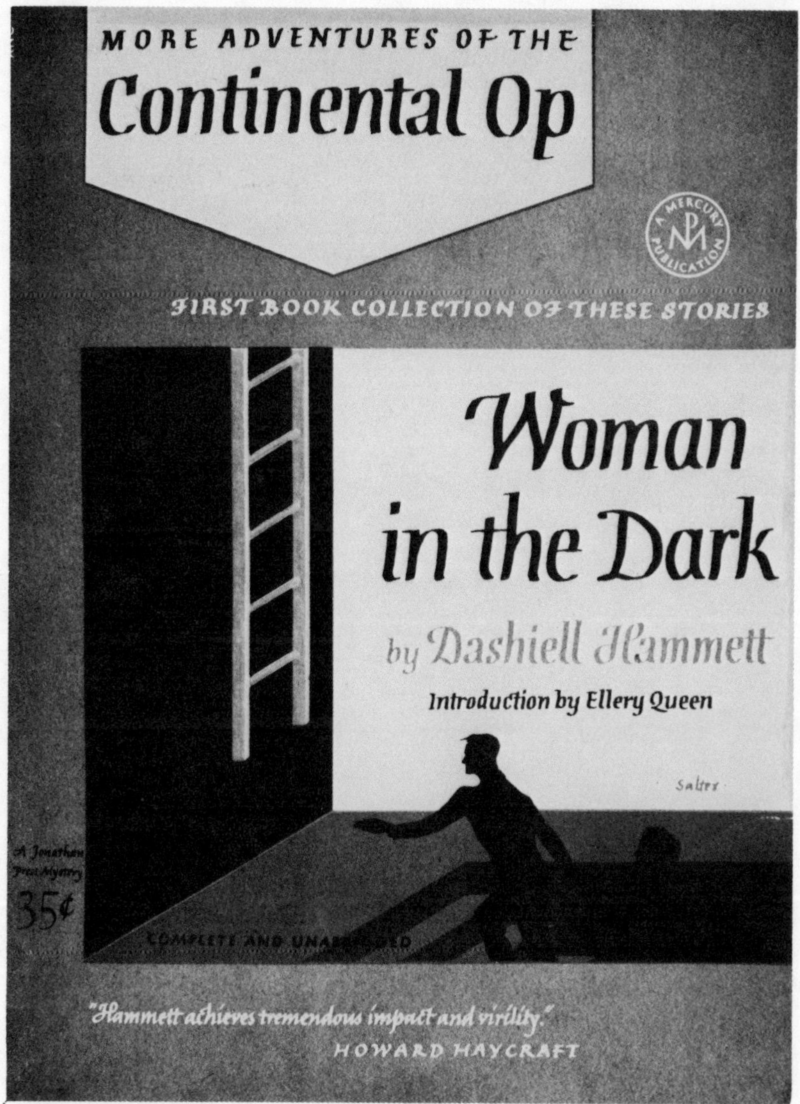

Front wrapper for A 18

COMPLETE AND UNABRIDGED | [white] *"Hammett achieves tremendous impact and virility." | HOWARD HAYCRAFT'*. Spine: '[vertically] [black] [swash] A [white] Dashiell Hammett [black] Detective [white] Woman in the Dark [black] A Jonathan Press Mystery [white] J 59'. Back: '[white] WOMAN IN THE DARK | [12-line advertisement] | [Mercury Publication seal]'. All edges trimmed.

Publication: Unknown number of copies of the first printing. 35¢. Published 25 June 1951. Copyright 25 June 1951. Copyright #A 271296.

Printing: Printing and binding by The Rumford Press.

Note: All stories in this volume were first published in magazines; see C 14, C 18, C 21, C 125, C 32, C 12, and C 9.

Locations: DLC ('JAN 14 1951'); OKentC; RL.

A19 A MAN NAMED THIN
Only edition (1962)

A MAN
NAMED THIN

and other stories by

DASHIELL HAMMETT

COMPLETE AND UNABRIDGED

Collected and edited,
with introduction and critical notes by
ELLERY QUEEN

Joseph W. Ferman, *Publisher*

A19: 7⅝" × 5⁵⁄₁₆"

Mercury Mystery No. 233

Mercury Press. Inc. 347 East 53rd Street New York 22, New York
© 1962, by Mercury Press, Inc.

Library of Congress Catalog Card Number: 62-11514
A Man Named Thin, © 1961 by Davis Publications, Inc.; In the Morgue, © 1923 by Inter-Continental Publishing Corp., renewed; all other stories, © 1922, 1923, 1921 by Dashiell Hammett, renewed.

Cover and design by George Salter

Perfect binding.

[3–5] 6–128 [129–130]

Contents: p. 3: title; p. 4: copyright; p. 5: contents; pp. 6–12: introduction by Ellery Queen; pp. 13–128: text; p. 129: blank; p. 130: blurbs by André Gide, Dorothy Parker, and *London Observer.*

Stories: "A Man Named Thin," *"Wages of Crime," *"The Gatewood Caper," *"The Barber and His Wife," *"Itchy the Debonair," *"The Second-Story Angel," *"In the Morgue," *"When Luck's Running Good." (Asterisks indicate first book publication.)

Typography and paper: 6 1/2″ (6 3/4″) × 4 1/8″. 35 or 36 lines per page. Running heads: rectos, story titles; versos, 'DASHIELL HAMMETT'. Wove paper.

Binding: Soft greenish blue wrappers. Front: '[black] PDC | [white] MERCURY MYSTERY | No. 233 [black Mercury Publications seal] | [white] 50¢ | [2 lines against white panel within very yellow panel, with alternating blue and black letters] A MAN | NAMED ['T', 'H', and 'N' in black; 'I' in blue] THIN | [2 lines against yellow panel] and other stories by | [script] Dashiell Hammett | [white] [roman] Edited and with introduction by | [script] Ellery Queen | *First book collection of these stories* | [yellow against deep green background] COMPLETE AND UNABRIDGED | [oval seal with drawing of running figure] *"Hammett achieves tremendous* | *impact and virility."* | *HOWARD HAYCRAFT*'. Spine: '[vertically] [white] DASHIELL HAMMETT A Man Named Thin *Mercury Mystery* [yellow against green background] *No. 233*'. Back: '[script] Dashiell Hammett | [16-line comment on Hammett from the *New York Times*]'. All edges trimmed.

Publication: Unknown number of copies of the first printing. 50¢. Published 19 January 1962. Copyright 19 January 1962. Copyright #A 550791.

Printing: Printed and bound by The Rumford Press and Philip Klein Lithography.

Note: All stories in this volume were first published in magazines; see C 136, C 7, C 17, C 4, C 25, C 22, C 16, and C 23.

Locations: DLC ('FEB 9 1962'); InU; RL.

MERCURY MYSTERY

No. 233

50c

A MAN NAMED THIN

and other stories by

Dashiell Hammett

Edited and with introduction by

Ellery Queen

First book collection of these stories

COMPLETE AND UNABRIDGED

"Hammett achieves tremendous impact and virility."

HOWARD HAYCRAFT

Front wrapper for A 19

A 20 THE BIG KNOCKOVER

A 20.1.a
First edition, first printing (1966)

THE BIG

Edited and with an
Introduction by
LILLIAN HELLMAN

KNOCKOVER

SELECTED STORIES
AND SHORT NOVELS OF

DASHIELL
HAMMETT

Random House
New York

A 20.1.a: two-page title; 11" × 8¼"

FIRST PRINTING

© Copyright, 1962, 1965, 1966, by Lillian Hellman
Copyright, 1924, 1925, 1926, 1927, 1929, by Pro-Distributors Company, Inc. © Copyright renewed, 1951, 1952, 1953, 1954, 1956, by Popular Publications, Inc.

All rights reserved under International and Pan-American Copyright Conventions. Published in New York by Random House, Inc., and simultaneously in Toronto, Canada, by Random House of Canada Limited.

Library of Congress Catalog Card Number: 66-18326

Manufactured in the United States of America

Designed by Jaime Davidovich

$[1-12]^{16}$

[i–vi] vii–xxi [xxii] [1–4] 5–355 [356–362]

Contents: p. i: blank; p. ii: card page; p. iii: half title; pp. iv–v: title; p. vi: copyright; pp. vii–xxi: introduction by Lillian Hellman; p. xxii: blank; p. 1: contents; p. 2: blank; p. 3: half title; p. 4: blank; pp. 5–355: text, headed 'The Gutting of Couffignal'; p. 356: blank; p. 357: biographical note on Hammett; pp. 358–362: blank.

Stories: "The Gutting of Couffignal," "Fly Paper," "The Scorched Face," "This King Business," "The Gatewood Caper," "Dead Yellow Women," "Corkscrew," *"Tulip," "The Big Knockover," "$106,000 Blood Money." (Asterisk indicates first book publication.)

Typography and paper: 6⁹/₁₆" (6¹³/₁₆") × 4³/₁₆". 43 lines per page. Running heads: rectos, story titles; versos, 'THE BIG KNOCKOVER'.

Binding: Black V cloth (smooth). Front: '[blindstamped] [Random House logo] | THE BIG | KNOCK- | OVER'. Spine: '[goldstamped] [Random House logo] | THE BIG | KNOCK- | OVER | DASHIELL | HAMETT | [in reverse printing against gold rectangle] RANDOM HOUSE'. Back: blank. White sized endpapers. Top and bottom edges trimmed. Top edge stained green.

Dust jacket: Green paper. Front: '[olive green] THE BIG | KNOCKOVER | [black] SELECTED STORIES AND SHORT NOVELS BY | [white] Dashiell Hammett | [black] EDITED AND WITH AN INTRODUCTION BY | [blue] LILLIAN HELLMAN | [drawing of human eye stylized to resemble falcon, with coffin]'. Spine: '[vertical] [dark green against olive background] THE BIG KNOCKOVER | by Dashiell Hammett | [horizontal] [white Random House logo] | [black against blue panel] RANDOM | HOUSE'. Back: '[black and white photo of Hammett] | [olive green against blue panel] Dashiell Hammett'. Front flap: '[37-line blurb about Hammett's work] | *Jacket design by Hoot Von Zitzewitz*'. Back flap: '[18-line biographical note on Hammett] | Random House, Inc. | 457 Madison Avenue, New York, New York 10022 | *Publishers of* The Random House Dictionary of the | English Language, The American College Dictionary | *and* The Modern Library | Printed in U.S.A.'. Dust jacket noted with and without '0364' on spine; priority uncertain.

Publication: Unknown number of copies of the first printing. $5.95. Copyright 1 June 1966. Published 1 June 1966. Copyright #A872382.

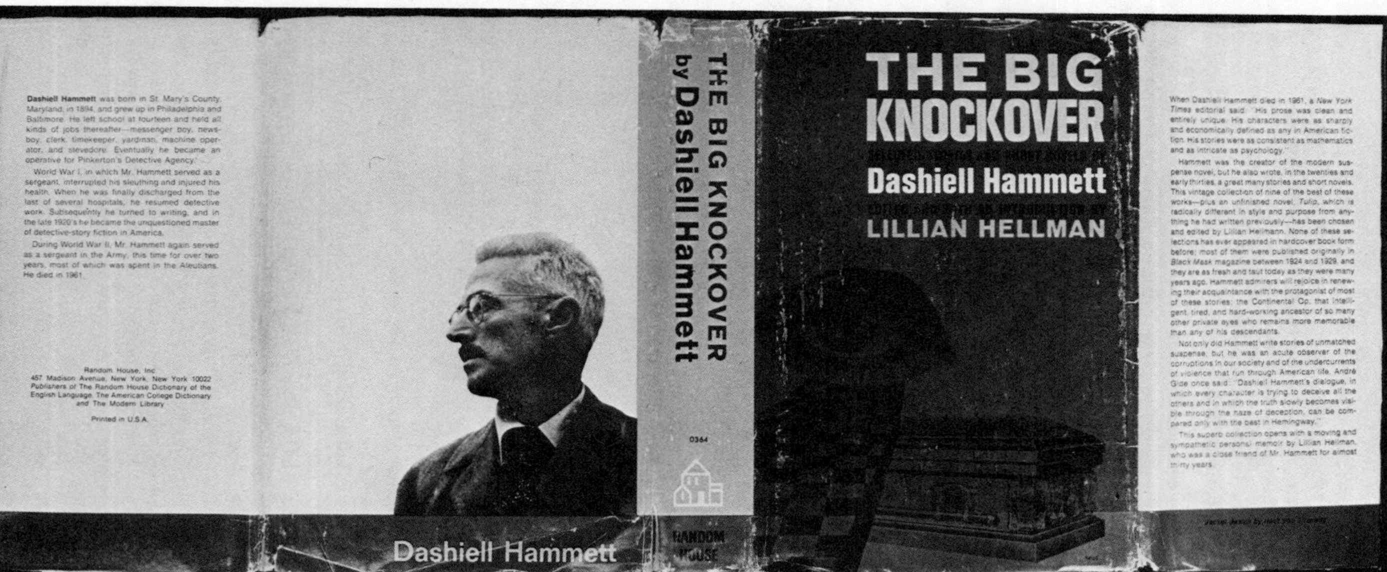

Dust jacket for A 20.1.a

Printing: Plates, printing, and binding by The Hadden Craftsmen.

Note: "Tulip" was first published in this volume. All other stories had been previously published in collections of Hammett's work; see C 59, C 106, C 52, C 82, C 17, C 58, and C 55.

Locations: DLC; InU (dj); RL (dj).

A 20.1.b
Second printing (1966)

Book-of-the-Month Club printing identified only by blindstamped square on lower right-hand corner of back binding. Dust jacket is identical with first-printing jacket that has '0364' on spine.

A 20.1.c
Third printing (1966)

The | DASHIELL | HAMMETT | Story | OMNIBUS | *Edited and with an Introduction by* | LILLIAN HELLMAN | [Cassell seal] | CASSELL • LONDON

Copyright page: 'F.766'.

A 20.2
Second edition (1967)

The Big | Knockover | [rule] | DASHIELL HAMMETT | A DELL BOOK.

Copyright page: 'First Dell Printing—July, 1967'.

5 stories: "The Gutting of Couffignal," "Fly Paper," "The Scorched Face," "Tulip," "The Big Knockover."

A 20.3
Third edition (1967)

[vertical rule on left margin] DASHIELL | HAMMETT | The | Continental | Op: | MORE STORIES | FROM | *THE BIG KNOCKOVER* | A DELL BOOK

Copyright page: 'First Dell Printing—December 1967'.

5 stories: "This King Business," "The Gatewood Caper," "Dead Yellow Women," "Corkscrew," "$106,000 Blood Money."

A 20.4
Fourth edition (1969)

The Big Knockover | and Other Stories | Edited and with an Introduction | by Lillian Hellman | Penguin Books.

1969. 10 stories. #C2941.

A 20.5
Fifth edition: Harmondsworth: Penguin, 1970.

Not seen.

A20.6
Sixth edition (1972)

The | *Big Knockover* | *Selected Stories and Short Novels of* | DASHIELL HAMMETT | *Edited and with an Introduction by* | LILLIAN HELLMAN | [Vintage seal] | VINTAGE BOOKS | A Division of Random House | NEW YORK

Copyright page: 'VINTAGE BOOKS EDITION, October 1972'.

A 21 BOOK REVIEWS
Only edition (1969)

Book Reviews
which appeared in
Saturday Review
Of Literature

by Dashiell Hammett

Portage, Indiana, 1969

A 21: $8^7/_8''$ × $5^5/_8''$

[1–4]^{8} [5]^{10} [6]^{6}

[i–x] 1–75 [76–78] 79–81 [82–86]

Contents: pp. i–ii: blank; p. iii: half title; p. iv: blank; p. v: title; p. vi: blank; p. vii: note; p. viii: blank; p. ix: half title; p. x: blank; pp. 1–74: text, headed 'January 15, 1927'; p. 75: note on Hammett's book reviews in *The Saturday Review;* p. 76: blank; p. 77: section title: 'Index'; p. 78: blank; pp. 79–81: index, headed 'AUTHOR INDEX'; pp. 82–86: blank.

Typography and paper: 4$^{13}/_{16}$" × 2$^{7}/_{8}$". Ragged right margin. No running heads. Coated paper.

Binding: Brown V cloth (smooth). Front and back blank. Spine: '[goldstamped] HAMMETT BOOK REVIEWS'. White wove sized endpapers. All edges trimmed.

Dust jacket: None.

Publication: Not for sale. Fewer than 30 copies. Produced as printing exercise.

Note: All sections previously published in *The Saturday Review of Literature;* see C68–C111 passim.

Location: RL.

A22 THE DIAMOND WAGER
Only edition (1977)

THE
DIAMOND
WAGER

by
SAMUEL DASHIELL

Portage, Indiana. 1977

A22: 11″ × 8½″

[1–4]^{6}. Unbound sheets.

[1–48]

Contents: pp. 1–4: blank; p. 5: title; p. 6: blank; p. 7: note about where story appeared and author; p. 8: blank; pp. 9–46: text; pp. 47–48: blank.

Typography and paper: 4¾″ × 6¼″. 25 lines per page. No running heads. Wove paper.

Publication: Not for sale. About 10 copies produced in Portage, Indiana, as a printing exercise.

Note: Previously published under the pseudonym Samuel Dashiell in *Detective Fiction Weekly;* see C 112.

Location: RL.

A 23 THE CONTINENTAL OP

A 23.1.a
First edition, first printing (1974)

DASHIELL HAMMETT

Selected and with an Introduction by
STEVEN MARCUS

A 23.1.a: $8^{3}/_{8}$″ × $5^{5}/_{8}$″

 Published in the United States by Random House, Inc., New York, and simultaneously in Canada by Random House of Canada Limited, Toronto.

Library of Congress Cataloging in Publication Data

Hammett, Dashiell, 1894–1961. The Continental Op.

CONTENTS: The tenth clew.—The golden horseshoe.—
The house in Turk Street. [etc.]
1. Detective and mystery stories, American.
I. Title.

PZ3.H1884Cq6 [PS3515.A4347] 813'.5'2 74–9050
ISBN 0–394–48704–4

Manufactured in the United States of America

9 8 7 6 5 4 3 2

FIRST EDITION

$[1–10]^{16}$

[i–viii] ix–xxix [xxx] [1–2] 3–38 [39–40] 41–81 [82–84] 85–108 [109–110] 111–160 [161–162] 163–214 [215–216] 217–242 [243–244] 245–287 [288–290]

Contents: p. i: blank; p. ii: card page; p. iii: half title; p. iv: blank; p. v: title; p. vi: copyright; p. vii: contents; p. viii: blank; pp. ix–xxix: introduction by Steven Marcus; p. xxx: blank; p. 1: section title; p. 2: blank; pp. 3–287: text; p. 288: blank; p. 289: biographical information about Hammett and Marcus; p. 290: blank.

Stories: "The Tenth Clew," "The Golden Horseshoe," "The House in Turk Street," "The Girl with the Silver Eyes," "The Whosis Kid," "The Main Death," "The Farewell Murder."

Typography and paper: 6⅛" (6½") × 3⅞". 34 lines per page. Running heads: rectos, '[story titles] | [rule]'; versos, 'THE CONTINENTAL OP | [rule]'. Wove paper.

Binding: Red boards quarter-bound in red V cloth (smooth). Front: '[blindstamped] THE CONTINENTAL OP [repeated in broken lines from top to bottom with a 4¼"-line length]'. Spine: '[goldstamped] [horizontal] DASHIELL | HAMMETT | [vertical] THE CONTINENTAL OP | [horizontal] [Random House logo] | RANDOM | HOUSE'. Back: blank. White sized endpapers. Top and bottom edges trimmed. Top edge stained yellow.

Dust jacket: Red paper. Front: '[yellow letters outlined in blue] DASHIELL | HAMMETT | [pink, blue, and brown drawing of man with gun and woman] | [white] THE | CONTINENTAL OP | EDITED AND WITH AN INTRODUCTION BY STEVEN MARCUS'. Spine: '[vertical] [yellow letters outlined in blue] DASHIELL HAMMETT | [white] THE CONTINENTAL OP | EDITED AND WITH AN INTRODUCTION BY STEVEN MARCUS | [horizontal] [Random House logo] | RANDOM | HOUSE'. Back: '[black and white photo of Hammett] | [white] PHOTO: EILEEN DARBY, GRAPHIC HOUSE 394-48704-4'. Front flap: '$7.95 | [26-line blurb]'. Back flap: '[14-line biographical note on Hammett; 10-line biographical note on Marcus] | Jacket design: Richard Mantel | Random House, Inc., New York, N.Y. 10022 | Publishers of the RANDOM HOUSE DICTIONARIES | The Modern Library and Vintage Books | Printed in U.S.A. | 11/74'.

Publication: Unknown number of copies of the first printing. $7.95.

Note: There are no first book publications in this volume.

Locations: DLC; InU (dj); RL (dj).

A 23.1.b
Second printing (1975)

Book-of-the-Month Club printing identified by blindstamped square on lower left-hand corner of back binding. Dust jacket same as for first printing except that it lacks price on front flap and '11/74' on back flap.

A 23.1.c
Third printing (1975?)

Copyright page: '9 8 7 6 5 4 3'.

A 23.2
Second edition (1975)

[within single-rule frame] THE | CONTINENTAL | OP [end frame] | DASHIELL HAMMETT | *Edited and with an introduction by* | STEVEN MARCUS | [Vintage seal] | VINTAGE BOOKS | A Division of Random House | New York

Copyright page: 'FIRST VINTAGE BOOKS EDITION, November 1975'.

#V-2013.

Dashiell Hammett was born in St. Mary's County, Maryland, in 1894. He left school at fourteen and held many jobs thereafter—messenger boy, newsboy, clerk, timekeeper, yardman, machine operator, and stevedore. He finally became an operative for Pinkerton's Detective Agency. After serving in World War I, he turned to writing, and in the late 1920's, became the unquestioned master of detective-story fiction in America. He was a sergeant in World War II. He died in 1961. Among his books are *The Big Knockover, The Dain Curse, The Glass Key, The Maltese Falcon, Red Harvest,* and *The Thin Man.*

Steven Marcus is a professor of English and Comparative Literature at Columbia University. Among his numerous writings are *Engels, Manchester & The Working Class* (1974), *The Other Victorians* (1966) and *From Pickwick to Dombey* (1965). He has also edited *The World of Modern Fiction* (1966), and with Lionel Trilling, Ernest Jones's *Life and Work of Sigmund Freud.* He is Associate Editor of *Partisan Review.*

Jacket design: Richard Mantel

Random House, Inc., New York, N.Y. 10022
Publishers of the RANDOM HOUSE DICTIONARIES,
The Modern Library and Vintage Books
Printed in U.S.A.
11/74

PHOTO: LILLIEN-DARBY, GRAPHIC HOUSE

394-48704-4

DASHIELL HAMMETT
THE CONTINENTAL OP
EDITED AND WITH AN INTRODUCTION BY STEVEN MARCUS

RANDOM HOUSE

DASHIELL HAMMETT

THE CONTINENTAL OP

EDITED AND WITH AN INTRODUCTION BY STEVEN MARCUS

$7.95

Dashiell Hammett is the great master and true inventor of modern detective fiction; the creator of the private eye, the isolated hero in a world where treachery is the only norm. These seven stories, which first appeared in the magazine *Black Mask* and have long been unavailable, are the best examples of Hammett's early writing, in which his formidable literary and moral imagination is already operating at full strength. They introduce the Continental Op, the dispassionate fat man from the Continental Detective Agency, an organization modeled on the Pinkerton Agency for which Hammett himself had worked. In these stories the reader will find the main themes of Hammett's later fiction—the skewed moral environment where nothing and no one can be trusted, the cold-eyed detective whose only interest is to do his job, and the criminals whose depravity mocks the pretensions of the reader's own world. These Continental Op stories create a world of violence and stealth, of cold passion, desperate action, and great excitement. They prefigure not only the world of subsequent detective fiction, but the world in which the contemporary reader actually lives.

Dust jacket for A 23.1.a

AA. Supplement

Collections

AA 1 DASHIELL HAMMETT OMNIBUS

AA 1.a

DASHIELL | HAMMETT | OMNIBUS | *Red Harvest • The Dain Curse* | *The Maltese Falcon* | [rule] | NEW YORK • ALFRED • A • KNOPF | *19* [Borzoi seal] *35*

Copyright page: *'Published August 12, 1935'.*

Contents: *Red Harvest, The Dain Curse, The Maltese Falcon,* all reprinted from first-edition plates.

AA 1.b

DASHIELL | HAMMETT | OMNIBUS | *Red Harvest • The Dain Curse* | *The Maltese Falcon* | [rule] | GROSSET & DUNLAP • Publishers | *by arrangement with Alfred A. Knopf*

Copyright page: Same as AA 1.a.

1937.

AA 1.c

[all within triple-rules frame] The Complete | Dashiell Hammett | [double rules] | THE THIN MAN • THE GLASS KEY | THE MALTESE FALCON | THE DAIN CURSE • RED HARVEST | [double rules] | NEW YORK: ALFRED • A • KNOPF | *19* [Borzoi seal within double ovals] *42*

Copyright page: *'Published July 20, 1942'.*

Contents: *Red Harvest, The Dain Curse, The Maltese Falcon, The Glass Key, The Thin Man,* all reprinted from first-edition plates.

AA 2 DASHIELL HAMMETT'S MYSTERY OMNIBUS

DASHIELL HAMMETT'S | MYSTERY OMNIBUS | CONTAINING TWO COMPLETE AND UNABRIDGED NOVELS | THE MALTESE FALCON and THE GLASS KEY | [Forum device] | CLEVELAND THE WORLD PUBLISHING COMPANY NEW YORK

Copyright page: 'FORUM BOOKS EDITION | *First Printing August, 1944* | [14 lines of type] | [battered letter] C'.

AA 3 THE DASHIELL HAMMETT OMNIBUS

AA 3.a

THE | Dashiell Hammett | OMNIBUS | [star] | THE THIN MAN | [star] | THE MALTESE FALCON | [star] | THE GLASS KEY | [star] | THE DAIN CURSE | [star] | RED

HARVEST | & | FOUR SHORT STORIES | [Cassell device] | CASSELL & CO. LTD | LONDON • TORONTO • MELBOURNE | SYDNEY • WELLINGTON

Copyright page: 'First published 1950 | SET IN 11 PT. BEMBO TYPE AND PRINTED IN GREAT BRITAIN BY | MORRISON AND GIBB LIMITED, LONDON AND EDINBURGH | F.450'.

Contents: Red Harvest, "Dead Yellow Women," *The Dain Curse,* "The Golden Horseshoe," *The Maltese Falcon,* "House Dick," *The Glass Key,* "Who Killed Bob Teal?," *The Thin Man.*

AA3.b
London: Cassell, 1952.

AA3.c
London: Cassell, 1953.

AA4 THE NOVELS OF DASHIELL HAMMETT

AA4.a

The Novels | OF | *Dashiell Hammett* | NEW YORK: *Alfred • A • Knopf*

Copyright page: 'THE NOVELS OF DASHIELL HAMMETT *was reset and printed from new plates.* | *Published October 1965'.*

Contents: Red Harvest, The Dain Curse, The Maltese Falcon, The Glass Key, The Thin Man.

AA4.b
Book-of-the-Month Club printing.

AA4.c
Third printing: New York: Knopf, 1966.

Copyright page: 'Reprinted June 1966'.

B. First-Appearance Contributions to Books

B 1 THE BEST AMERICAN MYSTERY STORIES
1932

The BEST | AMERICAN | MYSTERY | STORIES | *of the Year* | [rule] | *Selected and with an Introduction by* | CAROLYN WELLS | [rule] | *New York* | THE JOHN DAY COMPANY

"The Farewell Murder." See C 114.

B 2 THE BEST AMERICAN MYSTERY STORIES, TWO
1932

The BEST | AMERICAN | MYSTERY | STORIES | *of the Year* | [rule] | *Selected and with an Introduction by* | CAROLYN WELLS | [rule] | *Volume Two* | *New York* | THE JOHN DAY COMPANY

"Death and Company," pp. 3–17. See C 120.

B 3 THE SMART SET ANTHOLOGY
1934

[triple-rules frame at right and bottom edges of page] *The* | SMART SET | *Anthology* | *Edited by Burton Rascoe* | *and Groff Conklin* | REYNAL & HITCHCOCK | New York

"From the Memoirs of a Private Detective," pp. 85–89; "Green Elephant," pp. 463–471. See C 8 and C 20.

B 4 GOOD STORIES
1936

GOOD STORIES | *A collection adapted to the study* | *of the various phases of the short story* | EDITED BY | FRANK LUTHER MOTT | *Director, School of Journalism, State University* | *of Iowa* | [device] | NEW YORK | THE MACMILLAN COMPANY | 1936

Copyright page: 'Published November, 1936'.

"A Man Called Spade," pp. 441–476. See C 122.

B 5 WRITERS TAKE SIDES
1938

WRITERS TAKE SIDES | *Letters about the war in Spain* | *from 418 American authors* |

PUBLISHED BY | THE LEAGUE OF AMERICAN WRITERS | 381 FOURTH AVENUE, NEW YORK CITY

Copyright page: 'FIRST PRINTING, MAY, 1938'.

Statement by Hammett, p. 28.

B 6 FIGHTING WORDS
1940

FIGHTING WORDS | EDITED BY *Donald Ogden Stewart* | *hb* | HARCOURT BRACE AND COMPANY, NEW YORK

Copyright page: *'first edition'*.

Hammett speech quoted, pp. 53–57.

B 7 BEST STORIES FROM ELLERY QUEEN'S MYSTERY MAGAZINE
1944

Best Stories | FROM | *Ellery Queen's* | *Mystery Magazine* | SELECTED BY | ELLERY QUEEN | FOR THE READERS OF | *The Detective Book Club* | ONE PARK AVENUE • NEW YORK | *1944*

"Fly Paper," pp. 3–35. See C 106.

B 8 ROGUE'S GALLERY
1945

ROGUE'S | GALLERY | [device] | THE GREAT CRIMINALS | OF MODERN FICTION | [device] | EDITED BY | ELLERY QUEEN | [Little, Brown seal] | LITTLE, BROWN AND COMPANY • BOSTON | 1945

Copyright page: 'FIRST EDITION | Published October 1945'.

"Ruffian's Wife," pp. 7–23. See C 56.

B 9 WIND BLOWN AND DRIPPING
1945

WIND BLOWN | AND DRIPPING | A BOOK OF ALEUTIAN CARTOONS | By | CPL. BERNARD ANASTASIA | PFC. OLIVER PEDIGO | PFC. DON L. MILLER

3-page "Introduction" by Hammett, unpaged. Copy examined is in a private collection.

B 10 BEST FILM PLAYS OF 1943–1944
1945

[within single-rule frame and smaller decorated single-rule frame] [2 lines in hollow letters] BEST FILM PLAYS | OF 1943–1944 | *Edited by* | JOHN GASSNER | *and* | DUDLEY NICHOLS | [device] | CROWN PUBLISHERS | NEW YORK

"Watch on the Rhine," pp. 299–356. See E 6.

B 11 THE AVON ANNUAL
1945

[frame at top and right margin] THE AVON ANNUAL | [vertical list of 18 contributors against left margin] | 1945 | 18 | GREAT | MODERN | STORIES | AVON BOOK COMPANY | JO MEYERS E. R. WILLIAMS | 119 WEST 57TH STREET • NEW YORK

"To a Sharp Knife," pp. 57–69. See C 129 ("Two Sharp Knives").

B 12 THE ART OF THE MYSTERY STORY
1946

[within decorated double-rules frame] THE ART OF THE | MYSTERY STORY | A Collection of | Critical Essays | Edited and with a commentary by | HOWARD HAYCRAFT | [Simon and Schuster seal] SIMON AND SCHUSTER • New York • 1946

"The Benson Murder Case," pp. 382–383. See C 65 ("Poor Scotland Yard").

B 13 TWENTIETH CENTURY DETECTIVE STORIES
1948

Twentieth Century | Detective Stories | EDITED BY ELLERY QUEEN | ILLUSTRATED BY SEYMOUR NYDORF | FOURTEEN MODERN DETECTIVE STORIES | NEVER BEFORE PUBLISHED IN | BOOK FORM IN THE UNITED STATES | *including* "UNKNOWN" STORIES ABOUT | G. K. CHESTERTON'S Father Brown | DASHIELL HAMMETT'S Continental Op | AGATHA CHRISTIE'S Hercule Poirot | T. S. STRIBLING'S Professor Poggioli | *together with* QUEEN'S QUORUM | A READER'S AND COLLECTOR'S GUIDE TO | THE 101 MOST IMPORTANT BOOKS OF | DETECTIVE-CRIME SHORT STORIES, | WITH CRITICAL AND BIBLIOGRAPHICAL NOTES | *in short,* A SHORT HISTORY | OF THE DETECTIVE-CRIME SHORT STORY | CLEVELAND AND NEW YORK | THE WORLD PUBLISHING COMPANY

Copyright page: 'HCI'.

"Tom, Dick, or Harry," pp. 22–36. See C 48.

B 14 THE COMMUNIST TRIAL
1950

THE | COMMUNIST | TRIAL | *An American Crossroads* | by GEORGE MARION | FAIRPLAY PUBLISHERS | *25 West 44th Street* | *New York 18, N.Y.*

Copyright page: 'SECOND EDITION'.

"Introduction" by Hammett, p. [2].

Note: This is the second printing of the first edition; Hammett's introduction does not appear in the first printing.

Location: DLC.

B 15 PROCEEDINGS OF SENATE HEARING
1953

STATE DEPARTMENT INFORMATION PROGRAM— | INFORMATION CENTERS |

[double rules] | HEARING | BEFORE THE | PERMANENT SUBCOMMITTEE ON | INVESTIGATIONS OF THE COMMITTEE ON | GOVERNMENT OPERATIONS | UNITED STATES SENATE | 83D CONGRESS | 1st SESSION | PURSUANT TO | S. Res. 40 | A RESOLUTION AUTHORIZING THE COMMITTEE ON | GOVERNMENT OPERATIONS TO EMPLOY TEMPORARY | ADDITIONAL PERSONNEL AND | INCREASING THE LIMIT | OF EXPENDITURES | [short rule] | MARCH 24, 25, AND 26, 1953 | [short rule] | PART 1 | [short rule] | Printed for the use of the Committee on Government Operations | [device] | UNITED STATES | GOVERNMENT PRINTING OFFICE | 33616 WASHINGTON: 1953

Hammett testimony, pp. 83–88.

Location: RL.

B 16 THE BOYS IN THE BLACK MASK
1961

THE BOYS IN THE | [star] BLACK | MASK [star] | [left: man with revolver] | [right: mask] | AN EXHIBIT | IN THE | UCLA | LIBRARY | [below illustration] January 6–February 10, 1961

Cover title.

Note to first version of "The Thin Man," p. 8.

Location: OKentC.

B 17 ELLERY QUEEN'S 16TH MYSTERY ANNUAL
1961

ELLERY QUEEN'S | 16th MYSTERY | ANNUAL | The Year's Best | from *Ellery Queen's Mystery Magazine* | Edited by ELLERY QUEEN | [device] | RANDOM HOUSE • NEW YORK

"A Man Named Thin," pp. 221–242. See C 136.

B 18 WRITERS AT WORK
1967

[framed with vertical rule on either side, single row of devices at top, and 2 rows of devices separated by a single rule at bottom] • *Writers at Work* | [device] | *The Paris Review* Interviews | THIRD SERIES | *Introduced by Alfred Kazin* | NEW YORK: THE VIKING PRESS

Illustration of typescript page from Lillian Hellman's *The Little Foxes* with Hammett's holograph comments, p. 116.

B 19 AN UNFINISHED WOMAN
1969

AN UNFINISHED | WOMAN—*a memoir* | *by* Lillian Hellman | LITTLE, BROWN AND COMPANY • BOSTON • TORONTO | [Little, Brown seal] *with illustrations*

Copyright page: 'FIRST EDITION'.

Quotes and anecdotes concerning Hammett throughout.

B 20 A CATALOGUE OF CRIME
1971

A | CATALOGUE | OF | CRIME | SECOND IMPRESSION CORRECTED | *Jacques Barzun & Wendell Hertig Taylor* | [Harper & Row seal] HARPER & ROW, PUBLISHERS | NEW YORK, EVANSTON, SAN FRANCISCO, LONDON

Copyright page: 'SECOND IMPRESSION CORRECTED'.

Portion of Hammett letter to Blanche Knopf, 20 March 1928, quoted, p. 586.

B 21 LILLIAN HELLMAN PLAYWRIGHT
1972

[device] LILLIAN HELLMAN | *Playwright* | [device] | RICHARD MOODY | *Pegasus* [Pegasus device] New York | A DIVISION OF | *The Bobbs-Merrill Company, Inc., Publishers*

Copyright page: 'FIRST PRINTING'.

Quotes and anecdotes concerning Hammett throughout.

B 22 THE MYSTERY AND DETECTION ANNUAL
1972

THE | MYSTERY & DETECTION | ANNUAL | [drawing] | DONALD ADAMS | BEVERLY HILLS, CALIFORNIA | 1972

Copyright page: 'First printing'.

Donald K. Adams, "The First Thin Man," pp. 160–177, includes many quotes from the early "Thin Man" and a facsimile of Hammett's holograph headnote dated 'January 14, 1942'. See C 138.

B 23 PENTIMENTO
1973

PENTIMENTO | *A Book of Portraits* | *by* Lillian Hellman | LITTLE, BROWN AND COMPANY • BOSTON • TORONTO | [Little, Brown seal]

Copyright page: 'FIRST EDITION | TO9/73'.

Quotes and anecdotes concerning Hammett throughout.

B 24 SCOUNDREL TIME
1976

SCOUNDREL TIME | *by* Lillian Hellman | Introduction by Garry Wills | LITTLE,

BROWN AND COMPANY • BOSTON • TORONTO | [Little, Brown seal] *with photographs*

Copyright page: 'FIRST EDITION | TO 4/76'.

Quotes and anecdotes concerning Hammett throughout.

B 25 THE HARD-BOILED DETECTIVE STORIES
1977

THE | HARD-BOILED | DETECTIVE | STORIES | FROM | BLACK | MASK MAGAZINE | (1920–1951) | Edited, and | with an introduction, by | HERBERT RUHM | [Vintage seal] | VINTAGE BOOKS | A Division of Random House | New York

Copyright page: 'FIRST VINTAGE BOOKS EDITION, January 1977'.

"The Road Home," pp. 31–34. See C 5.

C. First Appearances in Periodicals

C 1
"The Parthian Shot." *The Smart Set,* 69, no. 2 (October 1922), 82.

Short short story.

C 2
"The Great Lovers." *The Smart Set,* 69, no. 3 (November 1922), 4.

Article.

C 3
"Immortality." *10 Story Book* (November 1922).

Story. Written as Daghull Hammett.

C 4
"The Barber and His Wife." *Brief Stories,* 7, no. 6 (December 1922), 23–29.

Story. Written as Peter Collinson. See *MNT* (A 19).

C 5
"The Road Home." *The Black Mask* (December 1922).

Story. Written as Peter Collinson. See B 25.

C 6
"The Master Mind." *The Smart Set,* 70, no. 1 (January 1923), 56.

Article.

C 7
"The Sardonic Star of Tom Doody." *Brief Stories,* 8, no. 2 (February 1923), 103–106.

Story. Written as Peter Collinson. Republished as "Wages of Crime" in *MNT* (A 19).

C 8
"From the Memoirs of a Private Detective." *The Smart Set,* 70, no. 3 (March 1923), 87–90.

Article. See B 3.

C 9
"The Vicious Circle." *The Black Mask,* 6, no. 6 (15 June 1923), 106–111.

Story. Written as Peter Collinson. Republished as "The Man Who Stood in the Way" in *WD* (A 18).

C 10
Letter. *The Black Mask,* 6, no. 6 (15 June 1923), 126–127.

C 11
"The Joke on Eloise Morey." *Brief Stories,* 8, no. 4 (June 1923), 295–298.

Story. See *CS* (A 17).

C 12
"Holiday." *The New Pearsons,* 49, no. 7 (July 1923), 30–32.

Story. See *WD* (A 18).

C 13
"The Crusader." *The Smart Set,* 71, no. 4 (August 1923), 9–10.

Story. Written as Mary Jane Hammett.

C 14
"Arson Plus." *The Black Mask,* 6, no. 13 (1 October 1923), 25–36.

Story. Written as Peter Collinson. See *WD* (A 18).

C 15
Letter. *The Black Mask,* 6, no. 13 (1 October 1923), 127.

C 16
"The Dimple." *Saucy Stories,* 15, no. 2 (15 October 1923), 115–116.

Story. Republished as "In the Morgue" in *MNT* (A 19).

C 17
"Crooked Souls." *The Black Mask,* 6, no. 14 (15 October 1923), 35–44.

Story. Republished as "The Gatewood Caper" in *MNT* (A 19).

C 18
"Slippery Fingers." *The Black Mask,* 6, no. 14 (15 October 1923), 96–103.

Story. Written as Peter Collinson. See *WD* (A 18).

C 19
Letter. *The Black Mask,* 6, no. 14 (15 October 1923), 127.

C 20
"The Green Elephant." *The Smart Set,* 73, no. 2 (October 1923), 103–108.

Story. See *DYW* (A 15), B 3.

C 21
"It." *The Black Mask,* 6, no. 15 (1 November 1923), 110–118.

Story. Republished as "The Black Hat That Wasn't There" in *WD* (A 18).

C 22
"The Second-Story Angel." *The Black Mask,* 6, no. 16 (15 November 1923), 110–118.

Story. See *MNT* (A 19).

C 23
"Laughing Masks." *Action Stories*, 3, no. 3 (November 1923), 61–81.

Story. Written as Peter Collinson. Republished as "When Luck's Running Good" in *MNT* (A 19).

C 24
"Bodies Piled Up." *The Black Mask*, 6, no. 17 (1 December 1923), 33–42.

Story. Republished as "House Dick" in *DYW* (A 15).

C 25
"Itchy." *Brief Stories* (January 1924).

Story. Written as Peter Collinson. Republished as "Itchy the Debonair" in *MNT* (A 19).

C 26
"The Tenth Clew." *The Black Mask*, 6, no. 19 (1 January 1924), 3–23.

Story. See *RCO* (A 13).

C 27
Letter. *The Black Mask*, 6, no. 19 (1 January 1924), 127.

C 28
"The Man Who Killed Dan Odams." *The Black Mask*, 6, no. 20 (15 January 1924), 35–41.

Story. See *CS* (A 17).

C 29
"Night Shots." *The Black Mask*, 6, no. 21 (1 February 1924), 33–44.

Story. See *HH* (A 14).

C 30
"The New Racket." *The Black Mask*, 6, no. 22 (15 February 1924), 34–37.

Story. Republished as "The Judge Laughed Last" in *ASS* (A 11).

C 31
"Esther Entertains." *Brief Stories*, 9, no. 6 (February 1924), 524–526.

Story.

C 32
"Afraid of a Gun." *The Black Mask*, 6, no. 23 (1 March 1924), 39–45.

Story. See *WD* (A 18).

C 33
"Zigzags of Treachery." *The Black Mask*, 6, no. 23 (1 March 1924), 80–102.

Story. See *CO* (A 12).

C 34
Two Letters. *The Black Mask*, 6, no. 23 (1 March 1924), 127–128.

C 35
Letter. *The Black Mask,* 6, no. 24 (15 March 1924), 127–128.

C 36
"One Hour." *The Black Mask,* 7, no. 1 (1 April 1924), 44–52.

Story. See *RCO* (A 13).

C 37
"The House in Turk Street." *The Black Mask,* 7, no. 2 (15 April 1924), 9–22.

Story. See *HH* (A 14).

C 38
"The Girl with the Silver Eyes." *The Black Mask* (June 1924).

Story. See *HH* (A 14).

C 39
Letter. *The Black Mask* (June 1924).

C 40
"In Defence of the Sex Story." *The Writer's Digest,* 4, no. 7 (June 1924), 7–8.

Article.

C 41
"Our Own Short Story Course." *The Black Mask,* 7, no. 6 (August 1924), 127–128.

Letter.

C 42
"Women, Politics and Murder." *The Black Mask,* 7, no. 7 (September 1924), 67–83.

Story. Republished as "Death on Pine Street" in *CO* (A 12).

C 43
"Mr. Hergesheimer's Scenario." *The Forum,* 72, no. 5 (November 1924), 720.

Book review.

C 44
"Who Killed Bob Teal?" *True Detective Stories,* 2, no. 2 (November 1924), 60–64, 93–95.

Story. See *DYW* (A 15).

C 45
"The Golden Horseshoe." *The Black Mask,* 8, no. 9 (November 1924), 37–62.

Story. See *DYW* (A 15).

C 46
Letter. *The Black Mask,* 7, no. 9 (November 1924), 128.

C 47
"Nightmare Town." *Argosy All-Story Weekly,* 165, no. 4 (27 December 1924), 502–526.

Story. See *NT* (A 16).

C 48
"Mike, Alec or Rufus." *The Black Mask* (January 1925).

Story. Republished as "Tom, Dick or Harry" in *CS* (A 17) and B 13.

C 49
"The Whosis Kid." *The Black Mask,* 8, no. 1 (March 1925), 7–32.

Story. See *RCO* (A 13).

C 50
"Ber-Bulu." *Sunset Magazine,* 54 (March 1925), 17–20.

Story. Republished as "The Hairy One" in *DYW* (A 15).

C 51
"Vamping Sampson." *The Editor,* 69, no. 6 (9 May 1925), 41–43.

Article.

C 52
"The Scorched Face." *The Black Mask* (May 1925).

Story. See *NT* (A 16).

C 53
"Finger-Prints." *The Black Mask,* 8, no. 4 (June 1925), 127–128.

Letter.

C 54
"Genius Made Easy." *The Forum,* 74, no. 2 (August 1925), 316–317.

Book review.

C 55
"Corkscrew." *The Black Mask* (September 1925).

Story. See *NT* (A 16).

C 56
"Ruffian's Wife." *Sunset Magazine* (October 1925).

Story. See *HH* (A 14), B 8.

C 57
"Caution to Travelers." *The Lariat* (November 1925), p. 507.

Poem.

C 58
"Dead Yellow Women." *The Black Mask* (November 1925).

Story. See *DYW* (A 15).

C 59
"The Gutting of Couffignal." *The Black Mask,* 8, no. 10 (December 1925), 30–48.

Story. See *RCO* (A 13).

C 60
"The Nails in Mr. Cayterer." *The Black Mask,* 8, no. 11 (January 1926), 59–73.

Story. See *CS* (A 17).

C 61
"The Assistant Murderer." *The Black Mask,* 8, no. 12 (February 1926), 57–59.

Story. See *ASS* (A 11).

C 62
"Creeping Siamese." *The Black Mask,* 9, no. 1 (March 1926), 38–47.

Story. See *CS* (A 17).

C 63
"The Advertisement Is Literature." *Western Advertising* (October 1926), pp. 35–36.

Article.

C 64
"The Cabell Epitome." *The Forum,* 77, no. 1 (January 1927), 159.

Book review.

C 65
"Poor Scotland Yard!" *The Saturday Review of Literature,* 3 (15 January 1927), 510.

Book review. See A 21, B 12.

C 66
"The Advertising Man Writes a Love Letter." *Judge* (26 February 1927), p. 8.

Parody.

C 67
"The Big Knock-Over." *Black Mask,* 9, no. 12 (February 1927), 7–38.[1]

Story. See *$106* (A 9).

C 68
Review of George Dilnot, *The Story of Scotland Yard. The Saturday Review of Literature,* 3 (19 March 1927), 668.

Book review. Anonymous.[2] See A 21.

C 69
"Yes." *Stratford Magazine,* 2, no. 2 (March 1927), 30.

Poem.

C 70
"Guessers and Deducers." *The Saturday Review of Literature,* 3 (16 April 1927), 734.

Book review. See A 21.

---

1. When Joseph T. Shaw became editor of *The Black Mask* in November 1926, he shortened the magazine's name to *Black Mask.*

2. Attributions to Hammett of anonymous book reviews in *The Saturday Review of Literature* are based on a list in the magazine's files of books sent to Hammett for review.

C 71
"Current Murders." *The Saturday Review of Literature,* 3 (21 May 1927), 846.

Book review. See A 21.

C 72
"$106,000 Blood Money." *Black Mask* (May 1927).

Story. See *$106* (A 9).

C 73
"Goodbye to a Lady." *Stratford Magazine,* 2, no. 5 (June 1927), 30.

Poem.

C 74
Review of Walter Gilkyson, *The Lost Adventurer. The Saturday Review of Literature,* 3 (11 June 1927), 901.

Book review. Anonymous. See A 21.

C 75
"The Main Death." *Black Mask,* 10, no. 4 (June 1927), 44–57.

Story. See *HH* (A 14).

C 76
"Curse in the Old Manner." *Bookman,* 66 (September 1927), 75.

Poem.

C 77
"The Cleansing of Poisonville." *Black Mask,* 10, no. 9 (November 1927), 9–37.

Excerpt from novel. See *RH* (A 1).

C 78
Review of Francis Carlin, *Reminiscences of an Ex-Detective. The Saturday Review of Literature,* 4 (10 December 1927), 439.

Book review. Anonymous. See A 21.

C 79
"Advertising Art Isn't Art—It's Literature." *Western Advertising* (December 1927), pp. 47–48.

Article.

C 80
"Crime Wanted—Male or Female." *Black Mask,* 10, no. 10 (December 1927), 9–33.

Excerpt from novel. See *RH* (A 1).

C 81
"Have You Tried Meiosis." *Western Advertising* (January 1928), pp. 60–61.

Article.

C 82
"This King Business." *Mystery Stories* (January 1928).

Story. See *CS* (A 17).

C 83
"Dynamite." *Black Mask,* 10, no. 11 (January 1928), 7–26.

Excerpt from novel. See *RH* (A 1).

C 84
Review of Edward H. Smith, *Mysteries of the Missing. The Saturday Review of Literature,* 4 (11 February 1928), 599.

Book review. Anonymous. See A 21.

C 85
"The Literature of Advertising—1927." *Western Advertising* (February 1928), pp. 154–156.

Article.

C 86
"The 19th Murder." *Black Mask,* 10, no. 12 (February 1928), 69–96.

Excerpt from novel. See *RH* (A 1).

C 87
"The Editor Knows His Audience." *Western Advertising* (March 1928), pp. 45–46.

Article.

C 88
Review of George Dilnot, *Great Detectives and Their Methods. The Saturday Review of Literature,* 4 (21 April 1928), 810.

Book review. Anonymous. See A 21.

C 89
Reviews of Henry Kitchell Webster, *The Quartz Eye;* John Stephen Strange, *The Man Who Killed Fortescue;* Rufus King, *The Fatal Kiss Mystery;* Frederick [*sic*] F. Van de Water, *Hurrying Feet;* Foxhall Daingerfield, *Wilderness House;* Dornford Yates, *Perishable Goods. The Saturday Review of Literature,* 5 (13 October 1928), 252.

Book reviews. Anonymous. See A 21.

C 90
Reviews of C. S. Forester, *The Daughter of the Hawk;* Edgar Wallace, *The Clever One. The Saturday Review of Literature,* 5 (20 October 1928), 282.

Book reviews. Anonymous. See A 21.

C 91
Reviews of Dorothy L. Sayers, *The Unpleasantness at the Bellona Club;* J. S. Fletcher, *The Shadow of Ravenscliff;* Augustus Muir, *The Shadow on the Left. The Saturday Review of Literature,* 5 (27 October 1928), 301.

Book reviews. Anonymous. See A 21.

C 92
"Black Lives." *Black Mask*, 11, no. 9 (November 1928), 41–67.

Excerpt from novel. See *DC* (A 2).

C 93
Reviews of Carolyn Wells, *The Tannahill Tangle;* J. S. Fletcher, *The Wrist Mark. The Saturday Review of Literature*, 5 (1 December 1928), 440.

Book reviews. Anonymous. See A 21.

C 94
Reviews of Maurice Renard and Albert Jean, *Blind Circle;* A. E. W. Mason, *The Prisoner in Opal. The Saturday Review of Literature*, 5 (8 December 1928), 492–493.

Book reviews. Anonymous. See A 21.

C 95
Review of Baroness Orczy, *Skin O' My Tooth. The Saturday Review of Literature*, 5 (22 December 1928), 543.

Book review. Anonymous. See A 21.

C 96
Review of Robert W. Sneddon, *Monsieur X. The Saturday Review of Literature*, 5 (29 December 1928), 559.

Book review. Anonymous. See A 21.

C 97
"The Hollow Temple." *Black Mask*, 11, no. 10 (December 1928), 38–64.

Excerpt from novel. See *DC* (A 2).

C 98
Review of H. C. McNiele, *The Female of the Species. The Saturday Review of Literature*, 5 (5 January 1929), 576, 578.

Book review. Anonymous. See A 21.

C 99
Reviews of Herman Landon, *Murder Mansion;* Wyndham Martyn, *Murder Island. The Saturday Review of Literature*, 5 (12 January 1929), 591.

Book reviews. Anonymous. See A 21.

C 100
Review of Clemence Dane and Helen Simpson, *Enter Sir John. The Saturday Review of Literature*, 5 (26 January 1929), 630.

Book review. Anonymous. See A 21.

C 101
"Black Honeymoon." *Black Mask*, 11, no. 11 (January 1929), 38–62.

Excerpt from novel. See *DC* (A 2).

C 102
Reviews of Richard Connell, *Murder at Sea;* Kay Burdekin, *The Burning Ring;* Jean Stark, *Phantom in the Wine;* J. J. Connington, *The Case with Nine Solutions. The Saturday Review of Literature,* 5 (9 February 1929), 669–670.

Book reviews. Anonymous. See A 21.

C 103
"Black Riddle." *Black Mask,* 11, no. 12 (February 1929), 40–67.

Excerpt from novel. See *DC* (A 2).

C 104
Reviews of Elizabeth Sanxay Holding, *Miasma;* Foxhall Daingerfield, *The Linden Walk Tragedy;* Charles Francis Coe, *Hooch. The Saturday Review of Literature,* 5 (27 April 1929), 961–962.

Book reviews. Anonymous. See A 21.

C 105
Review of Dorothy L. Sayers, *Lord Peter Views the Body. The Saturday Review of Literature,* 5 (4 May 1929), 983.

Book review. Anonymous. See A 21.

C 106
"Fly Paper." *Black Mask,* 12, no. 6 (August 1929), 7–26.

Story. See *CO* (A 12), B 7.

C 107
Review of Austin J. Small, *The Needle's Kiss. The Saturday Review of Literature,* 6 (7 September 1929), 116.

Book review. Anonymous. See A 21.

C 108
Review of John Rhode, *Murder at Bratton Grange. The Saturday Review of Literature,* 6 (21 September 1929), 164.

Book review. Anonymous. See A 21.

C 109
"The Maltese Falcon." *Black Mask,* 12, no. 7 (September 1929), 41–64; 12, no. 8 (October 1929), 31–52; 12, no. 9 (November 1929), 69–91; 12, no. 10 (December 1929), 69–91; 12, no. 11 (January 1930), 29–54.

Novel in parts. See *MF* (A 3).

C 110
Review of Armstrong Livingston, *The Monster in the Pool. The Saturday Review of Literature,* 6 (5 October 1929), 223.

Book review. Anonymous. See A 21.

C 111
Review of Ellery Queen, *The Roman Hat Mystery. The Saturday Review of Literature,* 6 (12 October 1929), 262.

Book review. Anonymous. See A 21.

C 112
"The Diamond Wager." *Detective Fiction Weekly,* 45, no. 2 (19 October 1929), 248–261.

Story. Written as Samuel Dashiell. See A 22.

C 113
Review of Jackson Gregory, *Mystery at Spanish Hacienda. The Saturday Review of Literature,* 6 (26 October 1929), 324.

Book review. Anonymous. See A 21.

C 114
"The Farewell Murder." *Black Mask,* 12, no. 12 (February 1930), 9–30.

Story. See *CO* (A 12), B 1.

C 115
"The Glass Key." *Black Mask,* 13, no. 1 (March 1930), 7–30.

Excerpt from novel. See *GK* (A 4).

C 116
"The Cyclone Shot." *Black Mask,* 13, no. 2 (April 1930), 45–70.

Excerpt from novel. See *GK* (A 4).

C 117
"Dagger Point." *Black Mask,* 13, no. 3 (May 1930), 50–72.

Excerpt from novel. See *GK* (A 4).

C 118
"The Shattered Key." *Black Mask,* 13, no. 4 (June 1930), 53–91.

Excerpt from novel. See *GK* (A 4).

C 119
"Behind the Black Mask." *Black Mask,* 13, no. 4 (June 1930), 119.

Letter.

C 120
"Death and Company." *Black Mask,* 13, no. 9 (November 1930), 60–65.

Story. See *RCO* (A 13), B 2.

C 121
"On the Way." *Harper's Bazaar* (March 1932), pp. 44–45.

Story.

C 122
"A Man Called Spade." *American Magazine,* 114, no. 1 (July 1932), 32–36, 92, 94–100.

Story. See *ASS* (A 11), B 4.

C 123
"Too Many Have Lived." *American Magazine,* 114, no. 4 (October 1932), 46–49, 94–98.

Story. See *ASS* (A 11).

C 124
"They Can Only Hang You Once." *Collier's,* 90, no. 21 (19 November 1932), 22–24.

Story. See *ASS* (A 11).

C 125
"Woman in the Dark." *Liberty,* 10, no. 14 (8 April 1933), 5–11; 10, no. 15 (15 April 1933), 12–18; 10, no. 16 (22 April 1933), 44–49.

Story. See *WD* (A 18).

C 126
"Night Shade." *Mystery League Magazine* (1 October 1933).

Story. See *ASS* (A 11).

C 127
"Albert Pastor at Home." *Esquire* (Autumn 1933), p. 34.

Story. See *NT* (A 16).

C 128
"The Thin Man." *Redbook* (December 1933), pp. 117–146.

Novel. See *TM* (A 6).

C 129
"Two Sharp Knives." *Collier's,* 93, no. 2 (13 January 1934), 12–13.

Story. See *HH* (A 14), B 11.

C 130
"His Brother's Keeper." *Collier's,* 93, no. 7 (17 February 1934), 10–11.

Story. See *ASS* (A 11).

C 131
"This Little Pig." *Collier's,* 93, no. 12 (24 March 1934), 10–11, 66–69.

Story.

Note

Beginning in May 1941 Hammett served on the editorial board of *Jewish Survey.*

C 132
"A Communication to All American Writers." *New Masses,* 42, no. 37 (16 December 1941), p. 22.

Public letter.

C 133
"The Thin Man and the Flack." *Click,* 4, no. 12 (December 1941), 30–32.

Photo story.

C 134
"Help Them Now." *New Masses,* 43, no. 7 (19 May 1942), 21.

Public letter.

C 135
Letter advertisement. *Soviet Russia Today* (October 1947).

C 136
"A Man Named Thin." *Ellery Queen's Mystery Magazine,* 37 (March 1961), 5–19.

Story. See *MNT* (A 19), B 17.

C 137
"Secret Agent X-9," *Captain George Presents,* 31–32 (1971?).

Entire double issue devoted to reprint of Hammett's comic strip. Includes all of *Secret Agent X-9 Book One* and a portion of *Book Two.* See *SA X-9* (A 7, A 8).

C 138
"The Thin Man." *City Magazine,* 9, no. 17 (4 November 1975), 1–12 (insert).

Story. This issue also includes numerous anecdotes about Hammett. See B 22.

UNDATED STORIES[3]

C 139
"The Man Who Loved Ugly Women." *Experience* (n.d., probably before May 1925).

Unlocated story.

C 140
"Another Perfect Crime." *Experience* (n.d., probably before May 1925).

Unlocated story.

C 141
"A Tale of Two Women." *Saturday Home Magazine* (n.d.).

Unlocated story. May be a retitled story syndicated by King Features.

C 142
"First Aide to Murder." *Saturday Home Magazine* (n.d.).

Unlocated story. May be a retitled story syndicated by King Features.

---

3. Entries C 139–C 142 are included on the basis of an inventory of Hammett's stories prepared by his secretary in the early 1950s.

D. First Appearances in Newspapers

Note: The following articles by Hammett were located while this bibliography was in page proof. The numbering designations indicate their positions in the chronological listing. These items are not included in the index.

THE ADAKIAN
1944–1945

D 406a
"Chicago Murder Mystery." 0, no. 3 (21 January 1944), 3.

D 406b
"Strictly Political." O, no. 5 (23 January 1944), 2.

D 408a
"Editorial Note." 1, no. 20 (18 February 1947), 4.

D 409a
"Apologies to 250 AC." 1, no. 38 (7 March 1944), 4.

D 410a
"Don't Let 'Em Kid You Into Buying War Bonds." 2, no. 80 (19 December 1944), 4.

Reprint of preceding article.

D 410b
Vol. 5, no. 29 (29 January 1945).

The first anniversary issue; includes a reprint of vol. 1, no. 1.

D 410c
"Home Sweet Home." 5, no. 77 (18 March 1945), Add Sunday leaf.

D 410d
"Home Sweet Home." 5, no. 84 (25 March 1945), Add Sunday leaf.

D 410e
"This Month's Payday Special." 5, no. 90 (31 March 1945), 3.

D 410f
"Rumors, Rumors, Rumors." 6, no. 1 (1 April 1945), Add Sunday leaf.

THE DAILY PRINCETONIAN

D 411a
"Dashiel [*sic*] Hammett Flees Night Club Round Succombing to Rustication in New Jersey." *The Daily Princetonian,* 11 November 1936, pp. 1, 4.

Interview.

NEW YORK EVENING POST[1]
1930

D 1
5 April 1930, p. M11.

Review of Mary Roberts Rinehart, *The Door.*

D 2
12 April 1930, p. M11.

Reviews of Philip MacDonald, *The Noose;* Ernest Sousa, *Blue Rum;* Virgil Markham, *The Black Door;* J. Jefferson Farjeon, *Following Footsteps.*

D 3
26 April 1930, p. M11.

Reviews of Anthony Berkeley, *The Wychford Poisoning Case;* Kay Cleavor, *Death Traps;* Bruce Graeme, *Through the Eyes of the Judge;* Claude Stuart Hammock, *Why Murder the Judge?;* Natalie Sumner Lincoln, *Marked "Cancelled.";* Frank Morrison, *Who Moved the Stone?;* "Diplomat," *Murder in the State Department.*

D 4
10 May 1930, p. M11.

Reviews of Gaston Leroux, *The Man of a Hundred Faces;* J. S. Fletcher, *The Yorkshire Moorland Murder;* Rupert Hughes, *Ladies' Man;* Leonard R. Gribble, *The Case of the Marsden Rubies;* H. Ashton-Wolfe, *The Forgotten Clue.*

D 5
24 May 1930, p. M8.

Reviews of S. S. Van Dine, *The Scarab Murder Case;* William Almon Wolff, *Manhattan Night;* N. A. Temple-Ellis, *The Man Who Was There;* Christopher Bush, *The Death of Cosmo Revere;* E. Phillips Oppenheim, *What Happened to Forester;* Victor K. Kaledin, *F-L-A-S-H D.13.*

D 6
7 June 1930, p. S4.

Reviews of Nancy Barr Mavity, *The Other Bullet;* Rayburn Crawley, *The Valley of Creeping Men;* Herman Landon, *The Voice in the Closet;* Helen Reilly, *The Thirty-First Bullfinch.*

---

1. Between 5 April 1930 and 11 October 1930 Hammett wrote a mystery-book-review column, "Crime Wave," for the *New York Evening Post.*

D 7
21 June 1930, p. M6.

Reviews of Eng Ying Gong and Bruce Grant, *Tong War!;* Sven Elvestad, *The Case of Robert Robertson;* J. Aubrey Tyson, *The Rhododendron Man;* Grace M. White and H. L. Deakin, *The Square Mark;* Tyline Perry, *The Owner Lies Dead;* Edgar Wallace, *The Green Ribbon;* Austin J. Small, *The Avenging Ray;* Alan LeMay, *One of Us Is a Murderer;* Mrs. Baillie Reynolds, *The Stranglehold;* David Frome, *The Hammersmith Murders;* Arthur A. Carey and Howard McLellan, *Memoirs of a Murder Man.*

D 8
3 July 1930, p. S5.

Reviews of Edgar Wallace, *The Hand of Power;* Anthony Wynne, *The Yellow Crystal.*

D 9
19 July 1930, p. S5.

Reviews of Raoul Whitfield, *Green Ice;* Lynn Brock, *Murder on the Bridge;* H. Ashbrook, *The Murder of Cecily Thane;* Basil King, *The Break of Day.*

D 10
2 August 1930, p. S5.

Reviews of Philip MacDonald, *The Link;* Sax Rohmer, *The Day the World Ended;* Stephen Chalmers, *The Affair of the Gallows Tree;* Sidney Horler, *Lady of the Night;* Van Wyck Mason, *Seeds of Murder;* Bertram Atkey, *The House of Strange Victims;* Francis Everton, *Murder Through the Window;* Laurence Meyneil, *The Mystery at Newton Ferry.*

D 11
23 August 1930, p. S5.

Reviews of William Averill Stowell, *The Marston Murder Case;* Milton Herbert Gropper and Edna Sherry, *Is No One Innocent?;* J. J. Connington, *The Two Ticket Puzzle;* Francis Beeding, *The Four Armourers;* Arthur Applin, *The Actress;* Sydney [*sic*] Horler, *The Curse of Doone;* Ian Greig, *The Silver King Mystery;* Murray Leinster, *Scalps;* Peter Baron, *The Opium Murders;* Elsa Barker, *The Redman Cave Murder;* Stuart Martin, *The Trial of Scotland Yard;* E. Phillips Oppenheim, *The Lion and the Lamb;* H. Ashton-Wolfe, *The Thrill of Evil.*

D 12
6 September 1930, p. S5.

Reviews of John Stephen Strange, *The Strangler Fig;* Robert J. Casey, *The Secret of the Bungalow;* Frederic F. Van de Water, *Alibi;* Thorne Smith, *Did She Fall?;* Roger Scarlett, *The Back Bay Murders;* Richard Keverne, *The Man in the Red Hat;* Marcus Magill, *I Like a Good Murder.*

D 13
20 September 1930, p. 12.

Reviews of Paul Selver, *Private Life;* S. Fowler Wright, *The Case of Anne Bickerton;* Octavus Roy Cohen, *The Backstage Mystery;* Vincent Starrett, *The Blue Door;* Mark Lee Luther and Lillian C. Ford, *The Saranoff Murder;* J. S. Fletcher, *The South Foreland Murder;* George Goodchild, *The Splendid Crime.*

D 14
11 October 1930, p. D4.

Reviews of H. C. Bailey, *The Garston Murder Case;* Victoria Lincoln, *The Swan Island Murders;* Edwin Dial Torgerson, *The Murderer Returns;* Selwyn Jepson, *I Met Murder;* Carolyn Wells, *The Ghosts' High Noon;* Earl Derr Biggers, *Charlie Chan Carries On.*

SECRET AGENT X-9[2]
1934–1935

D 15
29 January 1934, p. 13.

D 16
30 January 1934, p. 11.

D 17
31 January 1934, p. 11.

D 18
1 February 1934, p. 14.

Last two panels of this strip are omitted from *Secret Agent X-9* (A 7.1).

D 19
2 February 1934, p. 19.

D 20
3 February 1934, p. 12.

D 21
5 February 1934, p. 16.

D 22
6 February 1934, p. 16.

D 23
7 February 1934, p. 23.

D 24
8 February 1934, p. 18.

D 25
9 February 1934, p. 22.

D 26
10 February 1934, p. 12.

D 27
12 February 1934, p. 16.

D 28
13 February 1934, p. 22.

D 29
14 February 1934, p. 20.

D 30
15 February 1934, p. 22.

D 31
16 February 1934, p. 24.

D 32
17 February 1934, p. 12.

D 33
19 February 1934, p. 18.

D 34
20 February 1934, p. 18.

D 35
21 February 1934, p. 12.

D 36
22 February 1934, p. 16.

D 37
23 February 1934, p. 20.

D 38
24 February 1934, p. 12.

D 39
26 February 1934, p. 28.

2. *Secret Agent X-9* was a comic strip drawn by Alex Raymond and written by Hammett. It was syndicated by King Features. The strips are listed here as they appeared in the *San Francisco Call Bulletin.* See A 7.1 (prints D 15–D 89), A 7.2 (prints D 15–D 405), and A 8 (prints D 90–D 211).

D 40
27 February 1934, p. 18.

D 41
28 February 1934, p. 18.

D 42
1 March 1934, p. 18.

D 43
2 March 1934, p. 27.

D 44
3 March 1934, p. 12.

D 45
5 March 1934, p. 18.

D 46
6 March 1934, p. 18.

D 47
7 March 1934, p. 18.

D 48
8 March 1934, p. 11.

D 49
9 March 1934, p. 26.

D 50
10 March 1934, p. 12.

D 51
12 March 1934, p. 18.

D 52
13 March 1934, p. 23.

D 53
14 March 1934, p. 18.

D 54
15 March 1934, p. 20.

D 55
16 March 1934, p. 16.

D 56
17 March 1934, p. 12.

D 57
19 March 1934, p. 20.

D 58
20 March 1934, p. 20.

D 59
21 March 1934, p. 18.

D 60
22 March 1934, p. 18.

D 61
23 March 1934, p. 27.

D 62
24 March 1934, p. 14.

D 63
Entry canceled.

D 64
26 March 1934, p. 16.

D 65
27 March 1934, p. 12.

D 66
28 March 1934, p. 12.

D 67
29 March 1934, p. 22.

D 68
30 March 1934, p. 13.

D 69
31 March 1934, p. 16.

D 70
2 April 1934, p. 16.

D 71
3 April 1934, p. 18.

D 72
4 April 1934, p. 13.

D 73
5 April 1934, p. 17.

D 74
6 April 1934, p. 25.

D 75
7 April 1934, p. 12.

D 76
9 April 1934, p. 18.

D 77
10 April 1934, p. 16.

D 78
11 April 1934, p. 36.

D 79
12 April 1934, p. 18.

D 80
13 April 1934, p. 25.

D 81
14 April 1934, p. 12.

D 82
16 April 1934, p. 18.

D 83
17 April 1934, p. 20.

D 84
18 April 1934, p. 13.

D 85
19 April 1934, p. 18.

D 86
20 April 1934, p. 26.

D 87
21 April 1934, p. 12.

D 88
23 April 1934, p. 11.

D 89
24 April 1934, p. 18.

D 90
25 April 1934, p. 20.

D 91
26 April 1934, p. 28.

D 92
27 April 1934, p. 25.

D 93
28 April 1934, p. 12.

D 94
30 April 1934, p. 22.

D 95
1 May 1934, p. 18.

D 96
2 May 1934, p. 20.

D 97
3 May 1934, p. 26.

D 98
4 May 1934, p. 30.

D 99
5 May 1934, p. 12.

D 100
7 May 1934, p. 11.

D 101
8 May 1934, p. 16.

D 102
9 May 1934, p. 11.

D 103
10 May 1934, p. 26.

D 104
11 May 1934, p. 18.

D 105
12 May 1934, p. 12.

D 106
14 May 1934, p. 18.

D 107
15 May 1934, p. 16.

D 108
16 May 1934, p. 13.

D 109
17 May 1934, p. 18.

D 110
18 May 1934, p. 23.

D 111
19 May 1934, p. 12.

D 112
21 May 1934, p. 14.

D 113
22 May 1934, p. 9.

D 114
23 May 1934, p. 9.

D 115
24 May 1934, p. 25.

D 116
25 May 1934, p. 15.

D 117
26 May 1934, p. 12.

D 118
28 May 1934, p. 16.

D 119
29 May 1934, p. 9.

D 120
30 May 1934, p. 7.

D 121
31 May 1934, p. 22.

D 122
1 June 1934, p. 24.

D 123
2 June 1934, p. 12.

D 124
Entry canceled.

D 125
4 June 1934, p. 19.

D 126
5 June 1934, p. 8.

D 127
6 June 1934, p. 16.

D 128
7 June 1934, p. 18.

D 129
8 June 1934, p. 12.

D 130
9 June 1934, p. 13.

D 131
11 June 1934, p. 18.

D 132
12 June 1934, p. 14.

D 133
13 June 1934, p. 18.

D 134
14 June 1934, p. 20.

D 135
15 June 1934, p. 25.

D 136
16 June 1934, p. 12.

D 137
18 June 1934, p. 13.

D 138
19 June 1934, p. 17.

D 139
20 June 1934, p. 9.

D 140
21 June 1934, p. 16.

D 141
22 June 1934, p. 18.

D 142
23 June 1934, p. 12.

D 143
25 June 1934, p. 18.

D 144
26 June 1934, p. 9.

D 145
27 June 1934, p. 8.

D 146
28 June 1934, p. 22.

D 147
29 June 1934, p. 12.

D 148
30 June 1934, p. 10.

D 149
2 July 1934, p. 14.

D 150
3 July 1934, p. 6.

D 151
4 July 1934, p. 10.

D 152
5 July 1934, p. 20.

D 153
6 July 1934, p. 14.

D 154
7 July 1934, p. 10.

D 155
9 July 1934, p. 18.

D 156
10 July 1934, p. 16.

D 157
11 July 1934, p. 14.

D 158
12 July 1934, p. 18.

D 159
13 July 1934, p. 16.

D 160
14 July 1934, p. 6.

D 161
16 July 1934, p. 7.

D 162
17 July 1934, p. 10.

D 163
18 July 1934, p. 13.

D 164
19 July 1934, p. 6.

D 165
20 July 1934, p. 20.

D 166
21 July 1934, p. 8.

D 167
23 July 1934, p. 16.

D 168
24 July 1934, p. 14.

D 169
25 July 1934, p. 16.

D 170
26 July 1934, p. 19.

D 171
27 July 1934, p. 16.

D 172
28 July 1934, p. 16.

D 173
30 July 1934, p. 16.

D 174
31 July 1934, p. 16.

D 175
1 August 1934, p. 16.

D 176
2 August 1934, p. 20.

D 177
3 August 1934, p. 16.

D 178
4 August 1934, p. 10.

D 179
6 August 1934, p. 16.

D 180
7 August 1934, p. 14.

D 181
8 August 1934, p. 18.

D 182
9 August 1934, p. 18.

D 183
10 August 1934, p. 18.

D 184
11 August 1934, p. 16.

D 185
13 August 1934, p. 16.

D 186
14 August 1934, p. 14.

D 187
15 August 1934, p. 14.

D 188
16 August 1934, p. 8.

D 189
17 August 1934, p. 18.

D 190
18 August 1934, p. 10.

D 191
20 August 1934, p. 14.

D 192
21 August 1934, p. 14.

D 193
22 August 1934, p. 16.

D 194
23 August 1934, p. 20.

D 195
24 August 1934, p. 18.

D 196
25 August 1934, p. 16.

D 197
27 August 1934, p. 14.

D 198
28 August 1934, p. 14.

D 199
29 August 1934, p. 16.

D 200
30 August 1934, p. 10.

D 201
31 August 1934, p. 20.

D 202
1 September 1934, p. 10.

D 203
3 September 1934, p. 9.

D 204
4 September 1934, p. 14.

D 205
5 September 1934, p. 14.

D 206
6 September 1934, p. 22.

D 207
7 September 1934, p. 21.

D 208
8 September 1934, p. 10.

D 209
10 September 1934, p. 14.

D 210
11 September 1934, p. 10.

D 211
12 September 1934, p. 16.

D 212
13 September 1934, p. 24.

D 213
14 September 1934, p. 16.

D 214
15 September 1934, p. 10.

D 215
17 September 1934, p. 10.

D 216
18 September 1934, p. 11.

D 217
19 September 1934, p. 16.

D 218
20 September 1934, p. 12.

D 219
21 September 1934, p. 12.

D 220
22 September 1934, p. 12.

D 221
24 September 1934, p. 18.

D 222
25 September 1934, p. 12.

D 223
26 September 1934, p. 8.

D 224
27 September 1934, p. 21.

D 225
28 September 1934, p. 18.

D 226
29 September 1934, p. 12.

D 227
1 October 1934, p. 18.

D 228
2 October 1934, p. 14.

D 229
3 October 1934, p. 10.

D 230
4 October 1934, p. 21.

D 231
5 October 1934, p. 12.

D 232
6 October 1934, p. 12.

D 233
8 October 1934, p. 14.

D 234
9 October 1934, p. 10.

D 235
10 October 1934, p. 10.

D 236
11 October 1934, p. 12.

D 237
12 October 1934, p. 12.

D 238
13 October 1934, p. 12.

D 239
15 October 1934, p. 14.

D 240
16 October 1934, p. 14.

D 241
17 October 1934, p. 27.

D 242
18 October 1934, p. 12.

D 243
19 October 1934, p. 20.

D 244
20 October 1934, p. 12.

D 245
22 October 1934, p. 16.

D 246
23 October 1934, p. 14.

D 247
24 October 1934, p. 10.

D 248
25 October 1934, p. 23.

D 249
26 October 1934, p. 22.

D 250
27 October 1934, p. 12.

D 251
29 October 1934, p. 18.

D 252
30 October 1934, p. 18.

D 253
31 October 1934, p. 14.

D 254
1 November 1934, p. 23.

D 255
2 November 1934, p. 14.

D 256
3 November 1934, p. 12.

D 257
5 November 1934, p. 18.

D 258
6 November 1934, p. 8.

D 259
7 November 1934, p. 24.

D 260
8 November 1934, p. 14.

D 261
9 November 1934, p. 27.

D 262
10 November 1934, p. 12.

D 263
12 November 1934, p. 14.

D 264
13 November 1934, p. 14.

D 265
14 November 1934, p. 14.

D 266
15 November 1934, p. 14.

D 267
16 November 1934, p. 22.

D 268
17 November 1934, p. 12.

D 269
19 November 1934, p. 16.

D 270
20 November 1934, p. 14.

D 271
21 November 1934, p. 24.

D 272
22 November 1934, p. 28.

D 273
23 November 1934, p. 29.

D 274
24 November 1934, p. 12.

D 275
26 November 1934, p. 25.

D 276
27 November 1934, p. 24.

D 277
28 November 1934, p. 18.

D 278
29 November 1934, p. 15.

D 279
30 November 1934, p. 28.

D 280
1 December 1934, p. 12.

D 281
3 December 1934, p. 24.

D 282
4 December 1934, p. 20.

D 283
5 December 1934, p. 20.

D 284
6 December 1934, p. 30.

D 285
7 December 1934, p. 17.

D 286
8 December 1934, p. 12.

D 287
10 December 1934, p. 16.

D 288
11 December 1934, p. 16.

D 289
12 December 1934, p. 8.

D 290
13 December 1934, p. 28.

D 291
14 December 1934, p. 30.

D 292
15 December 1934, p. 12.

D 293
17 December 1934, p. 14.

D 294
18 December 1934, p. 18.

D 295
19 December 1934, p. 18.

D 296
20 December 1934, p. 28.

D 297
21 December 1934, p. 20.

D 298
22 December 1934, p. 12.

D 299
24 December 1934, p. 18.

D 300
25 December 1934, p. 15.

D 301
26 December 1934, p. 12.

D 302
27 December 1934, p. 20.

D 303
28 December 1934, p. 17.

D 304
29 December 1934, p. 12.

D 305
31 December 1934, p. 12.

D 306
1 January 1935, p. 12.

D 307
2 January 1935, p. 16.

D 308
3 January 1935, p. 13.

D 309
4 January 1935, p. 28.

D 310
5 January 1935, p. 12.

D 311
7 January 1935, p. 16.

D 312
8 January 1935, p. 16.

D 313
9 January 1935, p. 20.

D 314
10 January 1935, p. 20.

D 315
11 January 1935, p. 22.

D 316
12 January 1935, p. 12.

D 317
14 January 1935, p. 16.

D 318
15 January 1935, p. 18.

D 319
16 January 1935, p. 18.

D 320
17 January 1935, p. 29.

D 321
18 January 1935, p. 20.

D 322
19 January 1935, p. 26.

D 323
21 January 1935, p. 17.

D 324
22 January 1935, p. 16.

D 325
23 January 1935, p. 17.

D 326
24 January 1935, p. 24.

D 327
25 January 1935, p. 12.

D 328
26 January 1935, p. 12.

D 329
28 January 1935, p. 20.

D 330
29 January 1935, p. 18.

D 331
30 January 1935, p. 6.

D 332
31 January 1935, p. 30.

D 333
1 February 1935, p. 24.

D 334
2 February 1935, p. 12.

D 335
4 February 1935, p. 9.

D 336
5 February 1935, p. 19.

D 337
6 February 1935, p. 18.

D 338
7 February 1935, p. 25.

D 339
8 February 1935, p. 16.

D 340
9 February 1935, p. 12.

D 341
11 February 1935, p. 16.

D 342
12 February 1935, p. 16.

D 343
13 February 1935, p. 18.

D 344
14 February 1935, p. 29.

D 345
15 February 1935, p. 16.

D 346
16 February 1935, p. 12.

D 347
18 February 1935, p. 16.

D 348
19 February 1935, p. 16.

D 349
20 February 1935, p. 9.

D 350
21 February 1935, p. 6.

D 351
22 February 1935, p. 16.

D 352
23 February 1935, p. 12.

D 353
25 February 1935, p. 28.

D 354
26 February 1935, p. 20.

D 355
27 February 1935, p. 19.

D 356
28 February 1935, p. 37.

D 357
1 March 1935, p. 22.

D 358
2 March 1935, p. 12.

D 359
4 March 1935, p. 16.

D 360
5 March 1935, p. 18.

D 361
6 March 1935, p. 11.

D 362
7 March 1935, p. 29.

D 363
8 March 1935, p. 24.

D 364
9 March 1935, p. 12.

D 365
11 March 1935, p. 18.

D 366
12 March 1935, p. 16.

D 367
13 March 1935, p. 8.

D 368
14 March 1935, p. 25.

D 369
15 March 1935, p. 24.

D 370
16 March 1935, p. 12.

D 371
18 March 1935, p. 15.

D 372
19 March 1935, p. 16.

D 373
20 March 1935, p. 25.

D 374
21 March 1935, p. 12.

D 375
22 March 1935, p. 14.

D 376
23 March 1935, p. 12.

D 377
25 March 1935, p. 16.

D 378
26 March 1935, p. 16.

D 379
27 March 1935, p. 18.

D 380
28 March 1935, p. 17.

D 381
29 March 1935, p. 26.

D 382
30 March 1935, p. 12.

D 383
2 April 1935, p. 12.

D 384
3 April 1935, p. 22.

D 385
4 April 1935, p. 27.

D 386
5 April 1935, p. 18.

D 387
6 April 1935, p. 14.

D 388
8 April 1935, p. 11.

D 389
9 April 1935, p. 10.

D 390
10 April 1935, p. 29.

D 391
11 April 1935, p. 12.

D 392
12 April 1935, p. 28.

D 393
13 April 1935, p. 14.

D 394
15 April 1935, p. 8.

D 395
16 April 1935, p. 8.

D 396
17 April 1935, p. 27.

D 397
18 April 1935, p. 24.

D 398
19 April 1935, p. 26.

D 399
20 April 1935, p. 14.

D 400
22 April 1935, p. 10.

D 401
23 April 1935, p. 9.

D 402
24 April 1935, p. 13.

D 403
25 April 1935, p. 28.

D 404
26 April 1935, p. 12.

D 405
27 April 1935, p. 14.

THE ADAKIAN[3]
1944–1945

D 406
"It Happens to Everybody." 0, no. 1 (19 January 1944), 4.

D 407
"Editorial Note." I, no. 1 (29 January 1944), 4.

D 408
"War Bonds—At Home——And Here." 1, no. 17 (15 February 1944), 4.

D 409
"EM Mail." I, no. 23 (21 February 1944), 4.

D 410
"Don't Let 'Em Kid You Into Buying War Bonds." II, no. 35 (5 May 1944), 4.

OTHER NEWSPAPERS
1934–1961

D 411
"Author of Thrillers Is Sorry He Killed His Book Character." *San Francisco Call Bulletin*, 3 November 1934.

D 412
"500 Writers Ask 2D Front." *New York Times*, 15 September 1942, p. 46.

Statement by Hammett.

---

3. *The Adakian* was the post newspaper for the army base on Adak, Alaska. It was founded by Hammett in January 1944 and he was the editor until he was transferred from Adak in the spring of 1945. A trial issue headed "vol. 0, no. 1" was published on 19 January 1944; the first regular issue appeared on 29 January 1944. Because army regulations prohibited mailing the paper, copies are extremely scarce.

The Adakian was published 7 days a week in 3,000 to 6,000 copies. It was 4 pages, mimeographed. Typically the first 2 pages were devoted to international news and consisted of wire-service reports from the Associated Press, Army News Service, and Camp Newspaper Service; original news reports were based on foreign broadcasts monitored on WXLB, the Adak radio station. The last 2 pages consisted of camp news, movie schedules, radio schedules, and sports news. *The Adakian* staff consisted of 8 men, including 3 cartoonists, in addition to Hammett.

Articles are generally without bylines. Fifteen articles signed 'D.H.' have been located. Five of these, D 406–D 410, appear here. Ten others, which were located while this bibliography was in page proof, appear on page 138.

No institutional location for *The Adakian* has been found. Copies examined are from private collections.

D413
"Halt Anti-Negro Terror, City Asked." *Daily Worker*, 29 July 1946, p. 5.

Quotes open letter from Hammett.

D414
"Dashiell Hammett." *Daily Worker*, 12 March 1947, p. 3.

Statement by Hammett.

D415
"Peter V. Cacchione Dies." *Daily Worker*, 7 November 1947, p. 1.

Statement by Hammett.

D416
"Flay Purge." *Daily Worker*, 27 November 1947.

Statement by Hammett.

D417
"Hail Decision on Fired City Teacher." *Daily Worker*, 9 January 1948, p. 4.

Statement by Hammett.

D418
"Outlaws of the Old West." *New York Herald Tribune Book Review*, 27 November 1949, p. 12.

D419
"Dashiell Hammett Has Hard Words for Tough Stuff He Used to Write." *Los Angeles Times*, 7 June 1950.

D420
"Dashiell Hammett and Hunton Jailed in Red Bail Inquiry." *New York Times*, 10 July 1951, p. 1.

Statement by Hammett.

D421
"Hammett on Stand at Senate Book Witchhunt." *Daily Worker*, 27 March 1953, p. 3.

Statement by Hammett.

D422
James Cooper, "Lean Years for the Thin Man." *Washington Daily News*, 11 March 1957.

Quotes Hammett.

D423
"Dashiell Hammett, Author, Dies; Created Hard-Boiled Detectives." *New York Times*, 11 January 1961, p. 47.

Quotes Hammett.

D424
Leonard Lyons, "Tales About Hammett Told." *Hollywood Citizen-Reporter*, 19 January 1961.

Includes anecdotes about Hammett.

D425
"A Gentle Man Who Wrote About the Underworld." *Daily Worker*, 29 January 1961.

Statement by Hammett.

DD. Supplement

Public Letters or Petitions Signed by Hammett

DD 1
"Appeal for Lifting of Arms Embargo on Spanish Government." *Daily Worker,* 8 April 1938. p. 4.[1]

DD 2
"Leading Artist, Educators Support Soviet Trial Verdict." *Daily Worker,* 28 April 1938, p. 4.

DD 3
"Noted Liberals Call for Probe of Dies Committee." *Daily Worker,* 13 May 1940, p. 5.

DD 4
"Midwest Speeds Drive for C.P. Petition Names." *Daily Worker,* 3 August 1940, p. 4.

DD 5
"Save Lucy Carlos Prestes." *New Masses,* 37, no. 10 (26 November 1940), 22.

Open letter signed by Hammett and many others.

DD 6
"Rally Tonight to Protest Treatment of Refugee Jews." *Daily Worker,* 4 December 1940, p. 4.

DD 7
"Free Sam Darcy, Educators and Writers Urge Olson." *Daily Worker,* 19 December 1940, p. 5.

DD 8
"In Defense of Culture." *New Masses,* 39, no. 5 (22 April 1941), 25.

Call to Fourth Congress of the League of American Writers. Signed by Hammett and many others.

DD 9
"Worth Your Support." *New Masses,* 43, no. 7 (18 November 1941), 22.

Letter signed by 10 people including Hammett.

DD 10
"Eisler Indicted, Liberals Demand End of Persecution." *Daily Worker,* 28 February 1947, p. 2.

1. The *Daily Worker* referred to here was published in New York.

DD 11
"Noted Citizens Rap Attack on Communists." *Daily Worker,* 20 April 1947, p. 3

DD 12
"5,000 at Hollywood Rally Hit House Un-Americans." *Daily Worker,* 17 October 1947, p. 4.

DD 13
"Urge Truman Accept Stalin Bid." *Daily Worker,* 8 February 1949, p. 6.

DD 14
"70 Cultural Leaders Ask Truman-Stalin Talk." *Daily Worker,* 17 February 1949, p. 4.

DD 15
"33 American Writers Offer to Go Anywhere to Discuss Peace." *Daily Worker,* 14 March 1950, p. 10.

DD 16
"Writers Protest Videla Visit." *Daily Worker,* 10 April 1950, p. 2.

DD 17
"100 Notables Urge Talks by U.S., USSR on Korean War." *Daily Worker,* 7 August 1950, p. 8.

DD 18
"73 More Ask Bail for Communist '11'." *Daily Worker,* 24 August 1950, p. 3.

DD 19
"Notables Protest Attack on I.W.O." *Daily Worker,* 26 March 1951, p. 8.

E. Movies

E 1
City Streets, Paramount, 1931.

Screenplay by Oliver H. P. Garrett from adaptation by Max Marcin. Original story by Hammett.

E 2
Mister Dynamite, Universal, 1935.

Screenplay by Doris Malloy and Harry Clork. Original story by Hammett.

E 3
Satan Met a Lady, Warner Brothers, 1936.

Screenplay by Brown Holmes. Partially based on original story by Hammett.

E 4
After the Thin Man, Metro-Goldwyn-Mayer, 1936.

Screenplay by Frances Goodrich and Albert Hackett. Original story by Hammett.

E 5
Another Thin Man, Metro-Goldwyn-Mayer, 1939.

Screenplay by Albert Hackett and Frances Goodrich. Original story by Hammett.

E 6
Watch on the Rhine, Warner Brothers, 1943.

Screenplay by Hammett. See B 10.

Note

At the MGM studios in Culver City, California, there are 4 unpublished typescripts by Hammett as follows: (a) " 'After the Thin Man' (Thin Man Sequel)," 8 January 1935, 34 pp.; (b) " 'After the Thin Man' (Thin Man Sequel)," 17 September 1935, 115 pp.; (c) "Sequel to the Thin Man 'After the Thin Man,' " 7 December 1938, 8 pp.; and (d) "Another Thin Man," 13 May 1938 ("Recopied in Metro-Goldwyn-Mayer Script Department 8/17/39"), 144 pp.

F. Miscellaneous

F1

Nathanael West, *The Day of the Locust* (New York: New Directions, 1950).

New Classics #29. Dust-jacket blurb by Hammett on *The Day of the Locust*. (Also appears on dust jacket for *Miss Lonelyhearts* [New York: New Directions, 1950], New Classics #15.)

F2

A copy of a typed form letter dated 11 May 1938 addressed to F. Scott Fitzgerald is in the Fitzgerald archives at Princeton University Library. The letter asks support for liberal political candidates in the 1938 election.

Appendices / Index

Appendix 1

Ad Copy

From no earlier than 1922 to 1926 Dashiell Hammett wrote ad copy for the Albert S. Samuels Jewelry Company in San Francisco. This inventory includes all the Samuels ads that appeared in the *San Francisco Examiner.* It has not been established that Hammett wrote copy for any of these ads.

22 January 1922, p. 13.
29 January 1922, p. 6.
2 February 1922, p. 5.
5 February 1922, p. 18.
8 February 1922, p. 7.
12 February 1922, p. 10.
19 February 1922, p. 6.
26 February 1922, p. 12.
5 March 1922, p. 10.
12 March 1922, p. 10.
26 March 1922, p. 11.
2 April 1922, p. 11.
9 April 1922, p. 11.
16 April 1922, p. 11.
30 April 1922, p. 5.
28 May 1922, p. 7.
4 June 1922, p. 7.
11 June 1922, p. 7.
25 June 1922, p. 7.
9 July 1922, p. 7.
13 August 1922, p. 9.
1 October 1922, p. 7.
29 October 1922, p. 7.
5 November 1922, p. 9.
12 November 1922, p. 9.
19 November 1922, p. 7.
26 November 1922, p. 9.
3 December 1922, p. 13.
10 December 1922, p. 5.
17 December 1922, p. 6.
22 December 1922, p. 7.
23 December 1922, p. 7.
24 December 1922, p. 7.
31 December 1922, p. 5.
7 January 1923, p. 7.
14 January 1923, p. 7.
21 January 1923, p. 7.
28 January 1923, p. 7.
4 February 1923, p. 9.
4 March 1923, p. 7.
11 March 1923, p. 7.
18 March 1923, p. 7.
25 March 1923, p. 7.
1 April 1923, p. 7.
8 April 1923, p. 7.
15 April 1923, p. 7.
22 April 1923, p. 7.
29 April 1923, p. 6.
6 May 1923, p. 4.
13 May 1923, p. 7.
20 May 1923, p. 7.
27 May 1923, p. 7.
3 June 1923, p. 7.
10 June 1923, p. 7.
17 June 1923, p. 7.
24 June 1923, p. 7.
1 July 1923, p. 11.
8 July 1923, p. 6.
15 July 1923, p. 7
22 July 1923, p. 7.
29 July 1923, p. 7.
12 August 1923, p. 3.
13 August 1923, p. 3.
14 August 1923, p. 3.
15 August 1923, p. 3.
16 August 1923, p. 3.
17 August 1923, p. 3.
18 August 1923, p. 3.
19 August 1923, p. 3.
20 August 1923, p. 3.
21 August 1923, p. 3.
22 August 1923, p. 3.
23 August 1923, p. 3.
24 August 1923, p. 3.

26 August 1923, p. 7.
2 September 1923, p. 7.
9 September 1923, p. 7.
16 September 1923, p. 7.
30 September 1923, p. 7.
7 October 1923, p. 7.
14 October 1923, p. 7.
28 October 1923, p. 7.
4 November 1923, p. 4.
11 November 1923, p. 7.
25 November 1923, p. 7.
9 December 1923, p. 5.
16 December 1923, p. 8.
23 December 1923, p. 7.
20 January 1924, p. 7.
27 January 1924, p. 6.
3 February 1924, p. 15.
10 February 1924, p. 7.
24 February 1924, p. 7.
23 March 1924, p. 9.
6 April 1924, p. 7.
20 April 1924, p. 6.
27 April 1924, p. 4.
18 May 1924, p. 6.
25 May 1924, p. 11.
13 July 1924, p. 11.
16 July 1924, p. 2.
14 September 1924, p. 15.
19 October 1924, p. N3.
26 October 1924, p. N3.
9 November 1924, p. N3.
23 November 1924, p. N3.
30 November 1924, p. N3.
7 December 1924, p. N3.
14 December 1924, p. N3.
21 December 1924, p. N3.
28 December 1924, p. N3.
4 January 1925, p. N3.
11 January 1925, p. N3.
18 January 1925, p. 11.
23 January 1925, p. N3.
1 February 1925, p. N3.
8 February 1925, p. N3.
15 February1925, p. N3.
22 February 1925, p. 8.
1 March 1925, p. N3.
8 March 1925, p. N3.
15 March 1925, p. N3.
22 March 1925, p. N3.
29 March 1925, p. N3.
5 April 1925, p. N3.
12 April 1925, p. N3.
19 April 1925, p. N3.
26 April 1925, p. N3.
3 May 1925, p. N3.
8 May 1925, p. 5.
10 May 1925, p. N3.
17 May 1925, p. N3.
13 June 1925, p. 3
15 June 1925, p. 3.
17 June 1925, p. 4.
19 June 1925, p. 5.
22 June 1925, p. 3.
26 June 1925, p. 15.
9 August 1925, p. 17.
11 October 1925, p. 11.
18 October 1925, p. 11.
25 October 1925, p. 11.
1 November 1925, p. 13.
8 November 1925, p. 11.
15 November 1925, p. 15.
22 November 1925, p. 15.
29 November 1925, p. N5.
6 December 1925, p. 15.
13 December 1925, p. 13.
19 December 1925, p. 7.
20 December 1925, p. 15.
10 January 1926, p. 11.
17 January 1926, p. 11.
24 January 1926, p. 7.
31 January 1926, p. 11.
7 February 1926, p. 11.
21 February 1926, p. 2.
28 February 1926, p. 10.
7 March 1926, p. 13.
14 March 1926, p. 13.
21 March 1926, p. 10.
22 March 1926, p. 2.
28 March 1926, p. 15.
4 April 1926, p. 12.
30 May 1926, p. 9.
6 June 1926, p. 12.
20 June 1926, p. 12.
27 June 1926, p. 11.
4 July 1926, p. 11.
11 July 1926, p. 11.
18 July 1926, p. 8.[1]

1. Hammett resigned from the Albert S. Samuels Jewelry Co. on 20 July 1926.

Appendix 2

Radio Plays Based on Hammett's Work

2.1
The Thin Man, "Lux Radio Theater," 8 June 1936.

2.2
The Glass Key, "Campbell Playhouse," 1939.

2.3
After the Thin Man, "Lux Radio Theater," 17 June 1940.

2.4
The Adventures of the Thin Man, 2 July 1941 to 1 September 1950. NBC (1941–1942); CBS (1946–1948); ABC (1948–1950).

Series.

2.5
Two Sharp Knives, "Suspense," 22 December 1942.

2.6
The Glass Key, "Author's Playhouse," 29 January 1943.

2.7
The Maltese Falcon, "Lux Radio Theater," 8 February 1943.

2.8
The Maltese Falcon, "Screen Guild," 20 September 1943.

2.9
The Dain Curse, "Molle Mystery Theatre," 16 May 1944.

2.10
Two Sharp Knives, "Molle Mystery Theatre," 13 February 1945.

2.11
The Fat Man, 21 January 1946–1950. ABC (1946–1947); The Norwich Company (1947–1949); ABC (1949–1950).

Series.

2.12
The Glass Key, "Hour of Mystery," 7 July 1946.

2.13
The Adventures of Sam Spade, 12 July 1946–1951. CBS (1946–1949); NBC (1949–1951).

Series.

2.14
The Glass Key, "Screen Guild," 22 July 1946.

2.15
The Maltese Falcon, "Academy Award Theatre," July 1946.

2.16
The Glass Key, "Hollywood Players," 26 November 1946.

2.17
The Kandy Tooth Kaper, "Suspense," 17 November 1948.

2.18
The Maltese Falcon, "Screen Guild," 18 May 1950.

Appendix 3

Television Plays, Movies, and Stage Plays Based on Hammett's Work

3.1
Roadhouse Nights, Paramount, 1930.

Screenplay by Garrett Fort. Movie based on *Red Harvest.*

3.2
The Maltese Falcon, Warner Brothers, 1931.

Screenplay by Maude Fulton, Lucien Hubbard, and Brown Holmes. Movie.

3.3
The Thin Man, Metro-Goldwyn-Mayer, 1934.

Screenplay by Albert Hackett and Frances Goodrich. Movie.

3.4
Woman in the Dark, RKO Radio, 1934.

Screenplay by Sada Cowan. Movie.

3.5
The Glass Key, Paramount, 1935.

Screenplay by Kathryn Scola and Kubec Glasmon. Movie.

3.6
Shadow of the Thin Man, Metro-Goldwyn-Mayer, 1941.

Screenplay by Irving Beecher and Harry Kurnitz. Movie based on Hammett's *Thin Man* characters.

3.7
The Maltese Falcon, Warner Brothers, 1941.

Screenplay by John Huston. Movie (faithful adaptation of Hammett's novel).

3.8
The Glass Key, Paramount, 1942.

Screenplay by Jonathan Latimer. Movie.

3.9
The Thin Man Goes Home, Metro-Goldwyn-Mayer, 1944.

Screenplay by Robert Riskin and Dwight Taylor. Movie based on Hammet's *Thin Man* characters.

3.10
Song of the Thin Man, Metro-Goldwyn-Mayer, 1947.

Screenplay by Steve Fisher and Nat Perrin. Movie based on Hammett's *Thin Man* characters.

3.11
The Fat Man, Universal-International, 1951.

Screenplay by Harry Essex and Leonard Lee. Movie based on Hammett's character.

3.12
Cops, Yale Repertory Theatre, 1970.

Play adapted by Kenneth Cavander from story by Hammett.

3.13
Thin Man, "Movie of the Week," Universal, 1975.

3.14
The Dain Curse, CBS, 1978.

Movie made for television.

Appendix 4

Syndication of Previously Published Works by Hammett

KING FEATURES SYNDICATE

In January 1934 Hammett began an association with King Features Syndicate initiated by his *Secret Agent X-9* comic strip. First to promote the strip and later in a series of mystery fiction, King Features distributed at least 1 novel and 7 stories by Hammett, as listed below.

The Thin Man[1]

18 March 1934, p. 25.
19 March 1934, p. 17.
20 March 1934, p. 20.
21 March 1934, p. 19.
22 March 1934, p. 19.
23 March 1934, p. 25.
24 March 1934, p. 21.
25 March 1934, p. 17.
26 March 1934, p. 26.
27 March 1934, p. 30.
28 March 1934, p. 26.
29 March 1934, p. 22.
30 March 1934, p. 30.
31 March 1934, p. 21.
1 April 1934, p. E4.
2 April 1934, p. 26.
3 April 1934, p. 22.
4 April 1934, p. 30.
5 April 1934, p. 18.
6 April 1934, p. 27.
7 April 1934, p. 25.
8 April 1934, p. 20.
9 April 1934, p. 26.
10 April 1934, p. 28.
11 April 1934, p. 26.
12 April 1934, p. 26.
13 April 1934, p. 34.
14 April 1934, p. 26.
15 April 1934, p. 35.
16 April 1934, p. 16.

"Pick-Up" ("The Whosis Kid")[2]

4 April 1937, p. 5, section VII.
11 April 1937, p. 5, section VII.
18 April 1937, p. 5, section VII.

"The Girl with the Silver Eyes" (*mistitled publication of* "The House in Turk Street")[2]

25 April 1937, p. 5, section VII.
2 May 1937, p. 5, section VII.
9 May 1937, p. 5, section VII.
16 May 1937, p. 5, section VII.
23 May 1937, p. 5, section VII.

"The Girl Hunt" ("Flypaper")[2]

23 May 1937, p. 5, section VII.
30 May 1937, p. 5, section VII.
6 June 1937, p. 8, section VII.

"The Farewell Murder"[2]

6 June 1937, p. 8, section VII.

---

1. As it appeared in the *San Francisco Examiner.*

2. References are to first appearances in the *Washington Post.* These stories were syndicated as part of a series of mystery stories. After their initial distribution by King Features, they were periodically redistributed and appeared in various papers throughout the 1940s, including republication in the *Washington Post.*

13 June 1937, p. 8, section VII.
20 June 1937, p. 8, section VII.

"The Judge Laughed Last"[2]

20 June 1937, p. 8, section VII.

"Death and Co."[2]

27 June 1937, p. 8, section VII.

"The Second Story Angel"[2]

23 July 1937, p. 10, section VII.

HEARST NEWSPAPERS

In November 1934 evening newspapers in the Hearst chain carried "The Big Knock-over" in serial form. The serialization was examined in the *San Francisco Call Bulletin*, which carried a part of the story each day on the first page of the second section beginning on 11 November 1934.

SATURDAY HOME MAGAZINE

"The Golden Horseshoe" was serialized in *Saturday Home Magazine* on 21 July, 28 July, and 4 August 1938; "Girl Trap" ("The Scorched Face") appeared in September 1938. This magazine was a weekly supplement distributed with some of the Hearst newspapers.

Appendix 5

Compiler's Notes

The following are leads that have not been verified:

In early 1922 Hammett placed a want ad for a job in a San Francisco newspaper.

Hammett may have contributed to the *Haldeman-Julius Monthly* in the twenties.

It has been established that Hammett wrote ads on a free-lance basis between 1926 and about 1930, including a series of ads for a San Francisco shoe store, but none of these has been identified.

On 30 December 1936 Hammett wrote to Lillian Hellman that Wolcott Gibbs had sent him a one-dollar check for "that Raised Eyebrow Department Colony Club Contribution." No such item has been located in *The New Yorker*.

William F. Nolan reports in *Dashiell Hammett: A Casebook* that Hammett spent the last 6 months of his duty during World War II in Anchorage, Alaska, where he edited a monthly publication for "the Information and Education section."

New Ages for 9 February 1946 reportedly contains an article about Dashiell Hammett and the Jefferson School of Social Sciences. Magazine unlocated.

Hammett reportedly reviewed *Finnegans Wake* for *PM.*

Sometime before July 1947 Hammett is alleged to have written a pamphlet entitled "Radio Is Full of Gaps."

Hammett may have provided a statement in a book published as a tribute to New York City Councilman Benjamin J. Davis.

In March 1951 Hammett reviewed *Eyes of Reason* for the Liberty Book Club.

Hammett may have had a role in a pamphlet published by the Civil Rights Congress entitled *Whoever You Are.*

Appendix 6

Selected References

Gores, Joe. *Hammett*. New York: Putnam's, 1975.

Nolan, William F. *Dashiell Hammett: A Casebook.* Santa Barbara: McNally & Loftin, 1969.

———. "The Hammett Checklist Revisited." *The Armchair Detective,* August 1973, pp. 249–254.

———. "Revisiting the Revisited Hammett Checklist." *The Armchair Detective,* October 1976, pp. 292–295, 324–329.

Stoddard, Roger. "Some Uncollected Authors: XXXI Dashiell Hammett, 1894–1961." *The Book Collector,* 11, no. 1 (Spring 1962), 71–78.

Index

Pittsburgh Series in Bibliography

HART CRANE: A DESCRIPTIVE BIBLIOGRAPHY
Joseph Schwartz and Robert C. Schweik

F. SCOTT FITZGERALD: A DESCRIPTIVE BIBLIOGRAPHY
Matthew J. Bruccoli

WALLACE STEVENS: A DESCRIPTIVE BIBLIOGRAPHY
J. M. Edelstein

EUGENE O'NEILL: A DESCRIPTIVE BIBLIOGRAPHY
Jennifer McCabe Atkinson

JOHN BERRYMAN: A DESCRIPTIVE BIBLIOGRAPHY
Ernest C. Stefanik, Jr.

RING W. LARDNER: A DESCRIPTIVE BIBLIOGRAPHY
Matthew J. Bruccoli and Richard Layman

MARIANNE MOORE: A DESCRIPTIVE BIBLIOGRAPHY
Craig S. Abbott

NATHANIEL HAWTHORNE: A DESCRIPTIVE BIBLIOGRAPHY
C. E. Frazer Clark, Jr.

JOHN O'HARA: A DESCRIPTIVE BIBLIOGRAPHY
Matthew J. Bruccoli

MARGARET FULLER: A DESCRIPTIVE BIBLIOGRAPHY
Joel Myerson

RAYMOND CHANDLER: A DESCRIPTIVE BIBLIOGRAPHY
Matthew J. Bruccoli

DASHIELL HAMMETT: A DESCRIPTIVE BIBLIOGRAPHY
Richard Layman

Forthcoming

SUPPLEMENT TO F. SCOTT FITZGERALD: A DESCRIPTIVE BIBLIOGRAPHY
Matthew J. Bruccoli

JAMES GOULD COZZENS: A DESCRIPTIVE BIBLIOGRAPHY
Matthew J. Bruccoli